At Issue

Are Athletes Good Role Models?

Other Books in the At Issue Series:

At Issue

Are Athletes Good Role Models?

Kathy L. Hahn, Book Editor

GREENHAVEN PRESS
A part of Gale, Cengage Learning

GALE
CENGAGE Learning

Detroit • New York • San Francisco • New Haven, Conn • Waterville, Maine • London

Christine Nasso, *Publisher*
Elizabeth Des Chenes, *Managing Editor*

© 2010 Greenhaven Press, a part of Gale, Cengage Learning.

Gale and Greenhaven Press are registered trademarks used herein under license.

For more information, contact:
Greenhaven Press
27500 Drake Rd.
Farmington Hills, MI 48331-3535
Or you can visit our Internet site at gale.cengage.com

For product information and technology assistance, contact us at

Gale Customer Support, 1-800-877-4253
For permission to use material from this text or product, submit all requests online at
www.cengage.com/permissions

Further permissions questions can be e-mailed to permissionrequest@cengage.com

Articles in Greenhaven Press anthologies are often edited for length to meet page requirements. In addition, original titles of these works are changed to clearly present the main thesis and to explicitly indicate the author's opinion. Every effort is made to ensure that Greenhaven Press accurately reflects the original intent of the authors. Every effort has been made to trace the owners of copyrighted material.

Cover image reproduced by permission of Gstar.

LIBRARY OF CONGRESS CATALOGING-IN-PUBLICATION DATA

Are athletes good role models? / Kathy L. Hahn, book editor.
    p. cm. -- (At issue)
    Includes bibliographical references and index.
    ISBN 978-0-7377-4646-4 (hardcover) -- ISBN 978-0-7377-4647-1 (pbk.)
    1. Athletes--Conduct of life. 2. Role models. I. Hahn, Kathy L.
    GV706.8.A75 2010
    796.01--dc22

                                                                2009037394

Printed in the United States of America
1 2 3 4 5 6 7 13 12 11 10 09

Contents

Introduction

At first glance, George Herman "Babe" Ruth seems to be the unlikeliest of role models. Born into poverty, raised in a Baltimore orphanage, Ruth grew into a barrel-chested, spindle-legged man of average intelligence who loved chasing women, gulping hot dogs by the dozen, and swilling copious amounts of beer. A typical photo of the pug-nosed, overweight Ruth shows him with one arm circling a woman's waist, the other hand clutching a beer stein, and his lips wrapping a wide grin around a huge cigar.

But the Babe could play baseball, and could hit the seams off that ball; when he retired in 1935, his total home-run record of 714 round-trippers stood until Atlanta Brave Henry "Hank" Aaron topped him in 1974. His single-season record of 60, set in 1927, was not broken until 1961, when Yankee Roger Maris hit number 61 on the final day of that season. Although 26 years had passed since he had left the game, Ruth was still so beloved that Maris—a sleek, graceful athlete of high moral character—was booed and threatened by many fans, including those in New York, even though his hitting helped lead the Yanks to a World Series Championship that year!

Although the Babe was said to have had a heart as big as his belly, especially for children, he was also known for roughhousing, road antics and an attitude that today might be called in-your-face. Many of his characteristics might seem tame by today's standards, but times have changed considerably, and Ruth's "lovable" image might not be taken so lightly. In an age where open sexuality, obesity, tobacco, and alcohol abuse present huge challenges to young people, the role-model responsibilities of athletes have risen substantially—as has their exposure. Back in Ruth's era, the media was considerably more limited; newspaper/magazine articles, radio broadcasts, still photos, and an occasional movie reel were all that brought games to those who could not attend.

There was also a tacit understanding between the media and its coverage of the athletes; there were more boundaries established, less public invasion into the players' personal lives. Although a newsworthy and germane-to-the-game incident, such as the 1919 Chicago White Sox World Series scandal, would certainly be reported, what players did in their off time was kept in the locker room and/or in the pressroom. Reporters might wag tongues over their after-the-game nightcaps, but the gossip did not transcend into print or onto the radio airwaves the following day. As the century progressed, however, player salaries and residual income from commercial endorsements rose considerably, and the media expanded accordingly—as did public demand for information and accountability. If Ruth were playing today, he would have to drastically alter his larger-than-life image in order to be considered a true role model.

Remember, every major American sporting event today is attended by tens and tens of thousands—and this does not include the other thousands or even millions who visually tune in via worldwide television or streaming computer video, or listen to the old standby, radio play-by-play. For those who can't attend the game, sports bars and cafes offer large-screen coverage, and home televisions have become larger and offer ever greater high-definition clarity.

Gigantic high-definition pixels are not today's only watchdogs. The smallest camera screen can bring down the largest role model, and it does not have to be in the hands of a professional photojournalist or beat reporter to do its damage. As Olympic swimming champion Michael Phelps painfully learned, there are no "off the record" moments, and his brilliant, eight-gold-medal, 2008 Olympic performance—broadcast simultaneously worldwide and endlessly replayed—has been overshadowed by a quick cell phone snapshot of him smoking from a marijuana bong a scant three months after the Games were over. Following the Olympics, instead of relaxing and fading into a private lifestyle, Phelps chose to play his newfound fame to its fullest, and the same overexposure that came from lucrative commercial contracts and public appearances would also prove his undoing; he can no longer be considered a good role model. Endorsement offers have been revoked, and children are no longer urged to emulate him. In today's overhyped and report-saturated world, the ramifications of Phelps's misconduct reverberate far louder than any of the Babe's home-run smashes (or the resulting Yankee Stadium cheers) ever could.

Today's athlete has much to lose, financially and reputationwise, when he or she is found guilty of criminal activity and/or malfeasant behavior. Back when the Babe played there was little more than a ballgame (and a lot of self-esteem) on the line. But media scrutiny is a tough official scorekeeper, and very little happens in today's overmarketed and well-hyped sporting world that is not thoroughly analyzed and inspected. The authors of the viewpoints in *At Issue: Are Athletes Good Role Models?* examine the high-definition visibility of today's athletes, as well as other aspects of this controversial issue.

1

An Athlete Must Have Personal Integrity

R. Cort Kirkwood

R. Cort Kirkwood is the author of Real Men: Ten Courageous Americans to Know and Admire *and the managing editor of the* Daily News-Record *in Harrisonburg, Virginia.*

Lou Gehrig was one of the best baseball players of all time, yet it was his integrity, humility, and class, not his statistics, that made him a real man and a hero. Gehrig would have been out of place in modern sports, as he was not a criminal, did not have an ego, and was not arrogant and spiteful. Despite receiving a death sentence in the form of a diagnosis of amyotrophic lateral sclerosis, Gehrig still considered himself lucky and expressed his admiration for others when he was honored during Lou Gehrig Day at Yankee Stadium. Gehrig faced any challenge that came his way with integrity, which is no longer the case with most modern athletes.

No man is a hero to his wife. The aphorism is rooted in the seventeenth-century proverb, "No man is a hero to his valet," from Mademoiselle A. M. Bigot de Cornuel, an observation that, on meeting our heroes, we find they have feet of clay. Like us, they put their pants on one leg at a time.

But maybe that wasn't the case with Lou Gehrig, the man they called "Gibraltar in Cleats," mythic giant of the New York Yankees in the era of Ruth and Pipp and McCarthy and

R. Cort Kirkwood, "Batting a Thousand at Being a Man," *The New American*, August 7, 2006, pp. 34–38. Copyright © 2006 American Opinion Publishing Incorporated. Reproduced by permission.

Lazzeri. If any twentieth-century athlete qualifies as a man among men, it's Gehrig, the polar opposite of the modern athlete, represented in either the criminal, the crybaby, or the steroidally fortified multimillionaire. "He was beautiful," Eleanor Gehrig wrote. "Six feet tall, 205 pounds, sturdy as a rock and innocent as a waif."

The innocent waif was born June 19, 1903, Heinrich Ludwig Gehrig, into a rapidly changing world. Skyscrapers rose to the heavens in New York City. Henry Ford began the Ford Motor Company. Marie Curie won the Nobel Prize. Edwin S. Porter produced *The Great Train Robbery*. Thomas Hunt Morgan discovered chromosomes on genes, and the Wright Brothers flew. Other famous Americans born that year? Clare Boothe Luce, Bing Crosby, and Bob Hope. In England, George Orwell.

Gehrig's two sisters and a brother died before they reached the age of two. Lou's mother believed baseball was a "waste of time" that would "never get you anywhere," a "game for bummers." If you believe the film *Pride of the Yankees*, she wanted him to follow in the steps of his Uncle Otto, an engineer. Lou attended Columbia University on a football scholarship to study engineering, but he made his mark on the baseball diamond. It wasn't long before the Yankees came knocking, and in 1925, after a few years in the minors, Gehrig donned number 4. "Larrupin' Lou" batted fourth to Babe Ruth's third.

His statistics are legendary. He posted a lifetime .340 batting average and blasted 493 home runs. His batting average in the World Series was .361, with his best against Chicago in 1932, .529. Most impressive of all, he played 2,130 consecutive games, a record that stood until Cal Ripken of the Baltimore Orioles broke it on September 6, 1995. Gehrig played through broken fingers, sprained ankles, bruises, contusions, and just about every other imaginable ache and pain. X-rays showed seventeen broken or fractured bones in his hands, particularly the glove hand, many of which healed without the intervention of a doctor. He was one tough German.

All these facts about Gehrig add to his luster; they burnish his image as the kind of hero men can only dream of emulating. But it wasn't Gehrig's extraordinary athleticism that accounts for his inclusion here, nor is it why Gehrig is held in mythic regard. Rather, it was Gehrig's determined face while handling the adversity of a terminal disease.

Gehrig played ball for nearly fourteen years without a break, but in the season of 1938, his muscles began to fail. In *Pride of the Yankees*, it begins with a crick in his shoulder. Of course, he just shook it off. Just another day at the ballpark. But it was more than that.

The Iron Horse deteriorated rapidly. His teammates didn't know why, but they saw what was happening to this incredible specimen of manhood. His batting average plummeted 56 points to .295. A mystified Joe DiMaggio watched Gehrig miss nineteen straight cuts in batting practice. One afternoon he fell while trying to put on his pants in the clubhouse. Another time, he fell off a bench in the clubhouse when he got up to look out the window. Attending a pro-golf tournament in Florida, friends noticed he didn't wear cleats to walk in the grass as he usually would, but tennis shoes. He had good reason: he couldn't pick up his feet, which slowed his base running. Nor could he move his hands fast enough to catch balls fired across the diamond to him at first base. In the ultimate affront to a hitter of Gehrig's clout, a batter whose average hadn't dropped below .300 since 1925, Lefty Grove of the Boston Red Sox walked Joe DiMaggio so he could face the ailing first baseman. Gehrig was an easy out.

At home, Eleanor watched the decay, wondering what was happening to her Luke. Just a slump at the plate, they said. He just needs a little rest, everyone agreed. He dropped kitchen china inexplicably. He fell frequently when he and Eleanor went ice-skating, a favorite pastime. This, she asked herself, is a slump? Finally, on May 2, 1939, he took himself out of the lineup. A few weeks later, Eleanor scheduled an appointment at the Mayo Clinic. Dr. Harold Habein knew what was wrong as soon as Gehrig inched into his office. "When [he] entered my office," the doctor said, "and I saw the shuffling gait, and his overall expression, then shook his hand, I knew." The Iron Man had amyotrophic lateral sclerosis, after that, forever known as Lou Gehrig's disease. He was thirty-six.

The disease is a death sentence, although Lou didn't know right away. He died on June 2, 1941, sixteen years to the day he replaced Wally Pipp at first base.

A Modern Ballplayer

But before describing how Gehrig handled his tragic destiny, listen to another story about a modern ballplayer and how he handled what anyone would consider a disappointment, although certainly no colossal tragedy worthy of the rebarbative display to which the public was subjected.

The player's name is unimportant; it serves no purpose to ridicule the man. Let's just say he was, in his own mind, a player of Gehrig's caliber. He expected induction into the Baseball Hall of Fame.

Such was his conceit that he invited reporters to his home the day he knew the telephone call would come. They gathered in his kitchen, expecting, as did he, word of his elevation to baseball's Valhalla. But the news from Cooperstown wasn't what he expected, and he was not among the chosen few. Understandably, he was disappointed, as any good ballplayer would be. But he wasn't just disappointed. He was angry, feeling unjustly deprived of something he so richly deserved. What followed was a display of puerile histrionics: a foot-stomping, childish tantrum.

The *New York Times* reported: "[He] described how his wife . . . planned a surprise party for him and instead wept when they discovered he had not been elected. That caused [him] to cry, too. There were reporters [there] poised to witness a celebratory scene as he was finally honored as one of baseball's elite players. But it did not occur and tears flowed."

"He admitted to being devastated," the *Times* continued, "because he felt the expectation of being elected more than ever this year. He spoke about how it would torment him if his [aging father] did not live to see him enshrined." In complaining about the snub from baseball's pantheon of heroes, the player said, "I'd like to ask any of the sportswriters did any of them ever get behind the plate and catch for nine innings?"

When his batting average dropped, he took a three-thousand-dollar pay cut without complaint. He simply worked all the harder to recover his prowess at the plate.

Sitting behind a plate for nine innings? How about a death sentence before age forty? "Devastated"? You're "devastated" when your nine-year-old boy gets cancer. You're "devastated" when a drunk driver kills your daughter. But not when the Hall of Fame says it isn't your turn. What would Gehrig have said? Probably something like this: "Well, boys, you can't win 'em all. Let's toast the guys who made it. They were better men than me."

Since inducted at Cooperstown, the player is an example of modern American manhood, particularly the modern athlete, and we can thank the news media for depicting the specimen in all its glory. He is a perfect example of what we don't want our sons to be: conceited, arrogant, and spiteful, believing himself more deserving than someone else. Jesus Christ said the first will be last, and the last will be first. This fellow did not agree. One can only imagine how he would have handled the news Gehrig received in the flower of his manhood.

A Good Guy, a Great Man

Now, consider a few things about Gehrig, and you'll know he handled what most would say is a cosmic injustice and, in an unguarded moment, perhaps a divine injustice.

As with modern athletes, in the old days, an athlete's talents and popularity were measured in commercial endorsements. Lou endorsed a breakfast cereal called Huskies, and appearing on Robert Ripley's *Believe It or Not* radio program, he was supposed to plug the product. "Well, Lou, what helps you hit all those home runs?" Ripley asked.

"A heaping bowlful of Wheaties?" Lou replied. Huh? Wheaties? Lou returned the thousand dollars he was paid to pitch Huskies, then he returned to the show and plugged the cereal correctly.

"Lou," biographer Richard Bak wrote, "believed in doing the right thing." He invested all of his life savings for his parents after he married Eleanor and handed them the deed to a new house and new car.

Ever humble, even in his final appearance on the baseball diamond where he was a champion, he didn't speak of himself or his awful fate.

And we know he was tough. He played through those seventeen broken bones for more than a decade, including a thumb and toe, as well as back spasms, that would have dropped a less resilient man. He once played a game the day after a pitcher beaned him unconscious. Next day, he wore an oversized cap to accommodate the grapefruit on his noggin. He smashed three triples.

It wasn't easy for Gehrig to pull himself out of the lineup, but when he did, no one had to ask. He told manager Joe McCarthy: "For the good of the team, Joe. Nobody has to tell me how bad I've been and how much of a drawback I've been to the club. . . . [T]he time has come for me to quit." By all accounts, Gehrig was resolute and valiant. When his batting average dropped, he took a three-thousand-dollar pay cut without complaint. He simply worked all the harder to recover his prowess at the plate. He struggled mightily against the unknown. One account has Gehrig eating grass to conquer the creeping paralysis. Eleanor dutifully pulled it from the ground to make some sort of soup. He thought the vitamins would cure his disease. They didn't.

Gehrig Faces Death

On July 4, 1939, Gehrig delivered the most famous oration ever by an American athlete. Such was its emotive puissance it is known as baseball's Gettysburg Address. It was Lou Gehrig Day at Yankee Stadium, and all his teammates, current and former, were there to honor him. That included the Babe, with whom he hadn't spoken in years because Gehrig's mother (or wife, in some accounts) made an unflattering remark about the accouterments of Ruth's daughter. Sid Mercer, a veteran sportswriter who served as master of ceremonies, told the sixty thousand adoring fans that Gehrig was too moved to speak. The crowd wanted none of it. "We want Gehrig!" they roared. "We want Gehrig!" And Gehrig went to the microphone:

> Fans, for the past two weeks you have been reading about a bad break I got. Yet today, I consider myself the luckiest man on the face of the earth. I have been in ballparks for seventeen years and I have never received anything but kindness and encouragement from you fans.

Gehrig continued talking, but not about himself and his stellar career. Rather, he spoke about his teammates and pals and what they meant to him. And then he spoke about the men he played against, and how grateful he was that they sent him a gift. "That's something," he said. "Sure, I'm lucky."

That doesn't sound anything like the catcher who assembled sportswriters at his home to get the news about his induction into the Hall of Fame, but then hearing the bad news that he wasn't ready for Cooperstown, threw a tearful tantrum.

Gehrig's humility is one of the hallmarks of genuine masculinity. Ever humble, even in his final appearance on the baseball diamond where he was a champion, he didn't speak of himself or his awful fate. Rather, he told the assembled throng that he was lucky, then expressed his admiration for others, diverting the spotlight to them. He praised his mom and dad. He praised his loving wife. He even praised his adoring fans. He spoke about everyone but himself, and when he did speak of himself, it was only in the context of others: how lucky he was to have known them and for them to love him. Was he afraid? Undoubtedly. Eddie Rickenbacker said that courage is conquering fear, not the absence of it. Gehrig picked up the hand he was dealt and played it like a man.

Aside from showing us how a real man faces death, Gehrig was no criminal, as are so many of today's athletes. He was never convicted of a crime, nor ever accused of one. He never spit on an umpire or throttled his coach. He was no multimillion-dollar crybaby. Today, such "men" seem to be the rule, not the exception. Gehrig, a sportswriter once wrote, was "unspoiled, without the remotest vestige of ego, vanity or conceit."

One of Gehrig's teammates, shortstop Sam Jones, paid the Iron Man the highest compliment any man could hope to receive: "Lou was the kind of boy that if you had a son, he's the kind of person you'd like your son to be."

Likening him to the public image of the man who played him in *Pride of the Yankees*, Gary Cooper, another writer called him "a figure of unimpeachable integrity, massive and incorruptible, a hero. Today, both are seen as paradigms of manly virtue. Decent and God-fearing, yet strongly charismatic and powerful." The difference between the two, however, was that Gehrig genuinely embodied those traits.

Gehrig would be out of place in modern sports. It seems as if newspapers carry a daily report of millionaire athletes—particularly the rotten, criminal timber of the NBA [National Basketball Association] and the NFL [National Football League]—landing in jail. Few if any modern athletes are "innocent" or "massive and incorruptible" or "unimpeachable" or "unspoiled, without the remotest vestige of ego, vanity or conceit." Gehrig was.

One of Gehrig's teammates, shortstop Sam Jones, paid the Iron Man the highest compliment any man could hope to receive: "Lou was the kind of boy that if you had a son, he's the kind of person you'd like your son to be."

Any son's father knows what kind of tribute that is, the kind of tribute few modern athletes deserve. It says, in so many words, there goes a real man.

2

Parents Should Not Rely on Athletes as Role Models

Anthony Stalter

Anthony Stalter is a regular sports columnist for Bullz-Eye.com, an online magazine.

In a time when sports are widely televised and reported, it's easy (and tempting) for parents to encourage their children to emulate the athletes they see and hear so much about. What parents need to keep in mind, though, is that the feats performed on the playing field or court represent only a small part of who these athlete "heroes" really are, and what they might do or be involved with once the final whistle blows. All too often, parents rely on the positive image portrayed by someone whose athletic skills set him or her above the competition, which makes for confusion and a sense of betrayal when the role model turns out to be less than heroic.

It was Week 16 of the 2001 NFL [National Football League] season and the most talked about rookie in years lined up under center across from the Miami Dolphins defense.

Atlanta Falcons quarterback Michael Vick had taken over for Chris Chandler—who was knocked out of the game late in the first half due to an injury—and was trying to drive his team down the field trailing 21–7 late in the fourth quarter.

On a second and five from Miami's 49-yard line, Vick rolled out to his left and threw a 48-yard strike to receiver Shawn Jefferson, who was tackled at the one-yard line.

Anthony Stalter, "Barkley Had It Right All Along," *Bullz-Eye*, August 24, 2007. ©2000-2009 Bullz-Eye.com ®, All Rights Reserved. Reproduced by permission.

Vick threw the pass on one foot. Forty-eight yards ... one foot ... all arm. It was the most incredible throw I had ever seen in my life.

The Falcons wound up losing the game 21–14, but in that moment everyone who saw what Vick had done knew that he was going to be spectacular. I thought to myself, "He's going to be the face of the NFL and an athlete everyone will love and admire."

I've been wrong many times with sports predictions (just ask my editor Jamey Codding), but I don't think I could have been any more off base with my initial thoughts on Vick.

[Do] not allow your kids to solely look up to athletes as role models.

Little did I, nor anyone for that matter, know what Vick liked to do in his free time.

Athletes Are Typical Human Beings

In the mood for some light reading? Check out the 28-page federal indictment Vick was served for his participation in illegal gambling and dog fighting. Included in the document is the following:

> "... on or about June 29, 2001, Vick paid approximately $34,000 for the purchase of property located at 1915 Moonlight Road. .... From this point forward, the defendants used this property as the main staging area for housing and training pit bulls in the dog fighting venture and hosting dog fights."

On or about June 29, 2001? He was drafted April 22, 2001.

So basically he knew this was going to be his side project from day one—the thing that eventually cost him his career, his earnings and millions of supporters.

This will absolutely be the last time you read a column of mine dedicated to Michael Vick. In March [2007] I claimed I was sick of [troubled NFL player Adam] Pacman Jones and all of his antics, and thus I would never write more than a blog's worth of information on him again, which I haven't.

It doesn't make sense to keep wasting time talking about a human being that would rather dedicate his life to a sick hobby like dog fighting than to the rigors of professional football. But I feel inclined to shout from the rooftops a message to all parents—the message to not allow your kids to solely look up to athletes as role models.

Children Are Taught to Look Up to Athletes

Twenty years ago, if [former San Francisco Giant] Will "The Thrill" Clark had done something like this, I probably would have needed shock therapy to recover. But I'm old enough now to understand that, despite the money and the fame and the highlight reels, athletes are human beings, just like everyone else.

Yet when I recently drove past a local school playground, I saw not one but two young children running around with #7 "Vick" stitched onto their backs.

Which leads me to [former National Basketball Association player] Charles Barkley. He had it right when he said, "I am not a role model" during a 1993 commercial for Nike. Bear in mind that, during his NBA career, Barkley once spit on a nine-year-old girl at a game in 1991 (albeit the loogie was intended for a nearby heckler) and threw a man out of a window in Orlando [Florida]. It's also common knowledge that Chuck loves to gamble.

Barkley understood that parents shouldn't encourage their children to hold professional athletes up as role models, but he was criticized because people thought he meant athletes shouldn't *have* to be role models. That wasn't his message at all. It was more about parents taking responsibility for raising their children instead of thrusting that responsibility onto their hometown team's starting center fielder.

[NFL running backs] LaDainian Tomlinson, Warrick Dunn and [NY Yankee] Derek Jeter are just three athletes that I would encourage kids to look up to, but they alone shouldn't be counted on as role models. Instead, the actions of these players off the field should just be one of the many tools parents use to show their children the value of helping others.

Celebrate the fact that Dunn buys and furnishes homes for single mothers every year, but understand that he could turn around next week and get caught with a loaded weapon while driving under the influence.

Granted, that kind of situation would be completely out of character for Dunn, but that doesn't mean it couldn't happen. Would you have guessed that Vick enjoyed such a gruesome hobby this time last year? Don't forget, Vick was known as a quiet, polite and even painfully shy 20-year-old kid when he entered the NFL. He did an interview with *Sports Illustrated* early in his career and the writer insinuated that he had to use the Jaws of Life [equipment used to extract victims from wrecked vehicles and buildings] just to get the guy to talk.

You never know what these athletes are involved in once they step off the playing field.

Good Deeds Can Be Deceptive

He's done his fair share of charity work as well. In 2006, Vick, his mother Brenda Boddie and his knucklehead brother Marcus established the Vick Foundation, a nonprofit organization that supports at-risk youth and the after-school programs that serve them in Metro Atlanta. And after the tragic events at Virginia Tech earlier this year [in 2007], Vick . . . teamed with the United Way to help donate $10,000 to the victims' families. He also conducts an annual football camp for kids and was set to put on a charity golf tournament to raise scholarships in memory of the shooting victims at Tech before having to turn his attention to his court proceedings.

And through all of this, he helped drown, electrocute and hang dogs that did not perform well in fights.

But when the jerseys get hung up for the night, hopefully kids know that the people tucking them in are the real role models.

You never know what these athletes are involved in once they step off the playing field. That's why it's important that we be our kids' role models. Teach them the value of public service and helping others, and use the headlines from Tomlinson, Dunn and Jeter as examples. But don't forget Barkley's warning that athletes are just like everyone else. Yeah, they can dunk a basketball, hit a 400-foot home run or break off a 50-yard touchdown run, but when the lights fade, they breathe and bleed just like everyone else.

Parents Must Moderate and Lead by Example

It's easy to get caught up in the emotion and excitement that certain players bring to the field, which in turn will lead many parents to say to their children, "See Michael Vick? He's my favorite player and the best quarterback in the game!"

I'm not a psychologist but it only seems natural that, in trying to please mom and dad, some kids will adopt their parents' obsession for certain athletes as their own. They may start acting like the athlete on the field, talking like them and even dressing the same. Instead, they should be encouraged to be themselves on and off the playing field. That's not to say they shouldn't have favorite players. In fact, I grew up with #22 "Clark" [for former San Francisco Giants player Will

Clark] on my back. But when the jerseys get hung up for the night, hopefully kids know that the people tucking them in are the real role models.

That crazy Charles Barkley had it right all along.

3

There is Racial Disparity in Judging Athlete and Parent Role Models

David Leonard

David Leonard writes about sports.

African American male athletes, and their fathers, are held to different standards than their white counterparts by both the media and fans. A black athlete's behavior is subject to strict criticism, and his father's influence (or lack of same) is criticized even more harshly. There is no well-defined middle ground for how much input a black father should have on his son's professional career; the same commentators and columnists who chastise a father who stays out of his son's career choices are (at least) equally as judgmental when a father steps in and offers help or counsel. As members of a race long stereotyped for "absentee fatherism," concerned African American fathers of athletes are now being labeled as meddlesome and troublemaking.

In celebration of Father's Day last year [2005], FoxSports.com ran side-by-side articles on fathers, sons, and sports, chronicling the good and bad of various relationships. With "Athletes Whose Fathers Got them Started," [sports author] Elliot Kalb deployed the longstanding masculinized sporting clichés of fathers and sons (the lone woman included on this list was [tennis star] Monica Seles), celebrating those fathers "who coached and disciplined and taught and fought and influenced their children." To provide a "fair and balanced" counterpoint on fathers and athletes, the site published [sports writer] Kevin Hench's "The Domineering Dads that take the Cake." Like Kalb, Hench provided a list of fatherly influences on sports, but instead focused his attention on those relationships that "have not always produced a whole lot of hugs and presents on Daddy's big day."

The Winslow case once again demonstrates the ways in which sporting discourses and practices seek to control and discipline black bodies for optimal gain (and pleasure).

What struck me as I read the article was not so much the patriarchal inscription of sport, nor the overly simplistic notions of fathers rearing their children into sports (these are daily sports tropes that should surprise no one), but the absence of [former San Diego Charger tight end] Kellen Winslow Sr. from either list. While deserving, I found little shock in his absence from the list of fathers worth celebrating. However, given the widespread condemnation of both Winslow Sr. and his son, [the National Football League's] Cleveland Browns' tight end Kellen Jr., it is somewhat surprising that he did not find a place among overbearing figures like [basketball coach] Henry Bibby and [basketball star Kobe Bryant's father] "Jelly Bean" Bryant. Winslow Sr.'s ability to control his son has been repeatedly called into question by media and fans alike, replicating longstanding and ubiquitous practices of blaming black fathers as the source of familial and societal problems. Such questions materialized particularly following a motorcycle accident that left his son severely injured and the media salivating.

Black Athletes Are "Property"

It seemed to be just another average Sunday afternoon as Kellen Winslow Jr. sought to learn how to ride a motorcycle in a Canton, Ohio parking lot. Unfortunately, not all of the lessons took, with Winslow suffering injuries to his right shoulder and knee following an accident that threw him over the handlebars. Media and fans were criticizing Winslow Jr. even before he left the hospital. While it would be easy to reflect on other cases (LA Dodgers second baseman Jeff Kent, for one) where off-the-field activities resulted in injuries that prohibited on-the-field performance, it would be just as easy to examine how race has operated in the disparate coverage and level of outrage in these cases.

Throughout the sports pages and on the Internet, commentators denounced Winslow Jr. as yet another selfish, money-driven, lazy, self-centered basket case polluting sporting culture. Notwithstanding the amount of money Winslow has generated for both his employers (formerly the University of Miami and now the Cleveland Browns), his worth has been limited to his ability to perform on the field. Referred to as a jackass, a selfish (black) athlete, and an all-around bad guy for injuring himself on a motorcycle, the media and fans showed little compassion toward Winslow, reducing him to a piece of property worth nothing so long as he could not perform on the field. [Sports columnist] Rick Morrissey, in the *Chicago Tribune*, reminded the Winslow family and everyone else of this fact: "Winslow Jr. is ... the Browns' piece of property as much as a tackling dummy." Although I may not represent the working masses, I also certainly do not feel as if I am "the property" of my university. Nor do I think such rhetoric would resonate with the 9–5 sections of American life, except perhaps with the country's various sweatshop industries. The Winslow case once again demonstrates the ways in which sporting discourses and practices seek to control and discipline black bodies for optimal gain (and pleasure), with those transgressing the established boundaries finding themselves subjected to a series of disciplinary projects—opinion pieces, letters to the editor, and organizational efforts to recoup salary bonuses.

Accordingly, he was seen not as a good or nurturing father, but a corruptive element in his [son's] life.

Blacks Held to Different Standards

[Authors] C. Richard King and Charles Fruehling Springwood aptly link process of disciplinarity and sporting culture in "Body and Soul: Physicality, Disciplinarity, and the Overdetermination of Blackness," arguing that "Euro-American understandings of African Americans being excessive and transgressive have always fostered, if not demanded, disciplinarity, the application of regimes of control, regulation, and management." The level of outrage following Winslow's accident, like the panics induced by [then Minnesota Viking] Randy Moss's simulated "mooning" and the influx of high school kids into the NBA [National Basketball Association], reflects historic and racialized discourses of control, disciplinarity, and punishment of intruding, transgressing, and rule-breaking black bodies.

This outrage only intensified when, soon after the accident, Kellen Winslow Sr. took the media to task for its treatment of his son. "He made a mistake. You made it a circus. Remember when you were 21," Winslow rhetorically entreated. "A human being at 21 makes mistakes. He's not a piece of property." Not satisfied just defending his son, Winslow Sr. took this opportunity to blast the media for the level of coverage in this case and others. "You blow it out of proportion. This [shock TV show host] Jerry Springer mentality of journalism, you guys are better than that. You should be ashamed of yourselves." As [if to prove] Winslow Sr.'s point, the media propelled his comments into a national debate. ESPN and other media outlets described his comments as part of a "tirade," while an unidentified former player announced on NFL.com that the Hall of Famer should have known better.

Black Fathers Have Failed

Sports columnist Woody Paige, on ESPN's *Cold Pizza*, lambasted Winslow Sr. as a bad father who needed to dedicate more of his energies toward raising his son, rather than criticizing the media. [Sports commentator] Jay Marrioti, on the same network's *Around the Horn*, intimated that father and son were alike, and that his comments disgraced his legacy. Accordingly, he was seen not as a good or nurturing father, but a corruptive element in his [son's] life. Like Marrioti's, many of the attacks against Winslow Sr. did not just focus on his comments, but sought to demonize him as a father. Without evidence beyond a motorcycle accident and a few controversial interviews conducted by his *son* (one in which Winslow Jr., while at the University of Miami, had the nerve to compare the football field to a war zone after a 2003 game against Tennessee), one has to wonder on what grounds Winslow's fathering skills were being challenged.

Commentators denounced him as overbearing and meddling.

As of this writing, similar debates have not taken place regarding the failed efforts of the fathers of Jennifer Wilbanks (the "Runaway Bride"), [pregnant wife killer] Scott Peterson, [accused Dutch kidnapper/murderer of Natalie Holloway] Joran Van der Sloot, [ENRON CEO] Kenneth Lay, or a host of others. The attacks against Winslow Sr. recall those against [then San Francisco Giants' manager] Dusty Baker a few years ago, whose son, a batboy with the San Francisco Giants, was almost trampled during a playoff game, or Joe Jackson

(Michael's dad), whose overbearing and controlling parenting style has been cited as cause of Michael's "troubles." These criticisms demonstrate, as [author and professor of black popular culture] Mark Anthony Neal writes in *New Black Man*, "the significance we have placed in American society, and the black community specifically, on the relationship between fathers and their sons and on fatherhood and masculinity."

In his book, Neal reflects on the ways in which black fatherhood is rendered as absent and a source of problems for the black community within political/academic circles and popular culture projects. Black fatherhood in the media is seen as a national problem (as in the Moynihan report[, a 1965 government study titled "The Negro Family: The Case for National Action"]) or as an issue that young black males have to overcome (as in countless halftime pieces during the NBA finals), or both. Given the reduction of black fatherhood to explanations of communal and individual failings and the absence of representations of nurturing black fathers, it is no wonder that the media and various internet commentators focused on Winslow's failure as a father to make amends for his son's accident.

Black Fathers Promote Racism

The condemnation and outrage directed at the Winslow family is nothing new, though, as father and son found themselves in the media crosshairs during Jr.'s senior year in high school. As one of the most sought-after recruits in the nation, his decision regarding his college plans received much media coverage. After it became known publicly that Winslow Sr. did not want his son to sign with the University of Washington because of its lack of diversity, controversy erupted. Hoping to encourage his son to attend Michigan State University (who had a black coach at the time), Winslow Sr. gave Jr. the following advice: "I told him to take a look around. Thumb through the media guide and see how far you have to turn before you get to a person of color. And if you don't see people that look like you, there is a problem." Winslow Sr. took matters beyond advice, though, even refusing to sign his son's letter of intent to Washington. Although father and son eventually settled on the University of Miami, Winslow Sr. was widely criticized within the media, despite his son's public praise for his Dad's guidance. Commentators denounced him as overbearing and meddling. Others condemned his effort to insert race into his son's life, ostensibly instructing father not to play the race card with his son. To them, he was everything that Hench described as undesirable about sports fathers and worse, given that his actions did not merely create an unhappy father-son relationship, but helped form the dysfunctional behavior that Winslow Jr. had been taken to task over for the past three years.

Black Fathers Overly Scrutinized

Responding to this widespread critique, Black Coaches Association President Bob Minnix defended Winslow Sr., noting that, "The typical minority kid doesn't have a father like Kellen's to help in realiz[ing] all these things," to which Daniel Clark, an online commentator, responded: "Thank God." Winslow Sr., in Clark's estimation—and in the minds of many others—was not just a meddling sports Dad, but also a father facilitating a whole generation of immature black athletes [who] see bling and race before team and fundamentals. "No wonder the whole episode caused a rift within the Winslow family," wrote Clark sarcastically. "Kellen Sr. must have wondered where he'd gone wrong that his own son would fail to recognize where there were too many white people in his presence. So 'immature' [meant] that he'd shown none of his father's habitual suspicion and bitterness—but he's learning." Clark's tactic of "reverse racism" in his analysis of Winslow Sr.'s influence erases the reality of race in college athletics, as shown in the disparity between the large number of black athletes to the comparative lack of coaching and management positions filled by blacks. It is apparent in the popular responses to the Winslows' decisions that it is better for a (black) father to passively embrace the exploitation of his son for the "love of the game," rather than bring his son to consciousness where matters of race are concerned.

John Edgar Wideman, in his powerful memoir *Fatheralong*, explores the meaning of black fatherhood and seeks to challenge a "tradition of theft and distortion," working to reclaim his own and an entire community's generation of black fathers. "The stories must be told. Ideas of manhood, true and transforming, grow out of private, personal exchanges between fathers and sons," writes Wideman. "Yet for generations of black men in America this privacy, this privilege has been systematically breached in a most shameful and public way. Not only breached, but brutally usurped, mediated by murder, mayhem, and misinformation." Whether it be narratives that articulate national concern (panic) for the "absentee black father" as the source of (black) societal problems, or media and discursive efforts to demonize and police black fathers, these assertions demonstrate the persistent question that remains within the American psyche: is black fatherhood an oxymoron? The media and fan condemnation of Kellen Winslow Sr. (and Jr.) provides insight into this answer. Now, that is shameful.

4

Failures of Role-Model Athletes Do Not Diminish Interest in Sports

Jack McCallum

Jack McCallum started writing for Sports Illustrated *in 1981 and has been that magazine's chief National Basketball Association writer since 1985. In 2004, he won the Basketball Hall of Fame's Curt Gowdy Media Award for outstanding writing. He is the author of* Unfinished Business: On and Off the Court with the 1990–91 Boston Celtics *and coauthor of* Foul Lines: A Pro Basketball Novel.

Despite a seeming upturn of poor behavior among athletic role models, fan interest has not lessened; it has, in fact, grown. The commerciality and profitability of a big-name athlete may or may not dwindle when he or she misbehaves or cheats; however, the increased media attention, whether positive or negative, often serves to bring more interest—and thus potential financial gain—to that athlete and his or her particular sport. As long as profitability remains, even if stoked by controversy, businesses will continue to invest in athletes and athletic-related ventures.

A man wearing a white number 7 Michael Vick replica jersey stood defiantly in the gallery of a federal courtroom in Richmond last Thursday [August 2, 2007] as the Atlanta Falcons' star quarterback pleaded not guilty to charges related to dogfighting. Whatever you think about the spectator, Shawn

Dodson of Lynchburg, Va., the man has a thick skin. As he left the courtroom following the hearing, the 33-year-old Dodson was jeered by pet owners and animal-rights activists and other wide swaths of the citizenry. "This is crazy," he said.

Some would say that showing support for a 27-year-old multimillionaire who allegedly took part in killing his under-performing dogs by electrocution and drowning is crazy. But the circus atmosphere that surrounded the Vick hearing, as well as subsequent comments about the dogfighting case, prove one thing: In America there are always divergent points of view.[1]

Well, almost always. A Save Tim Donaghy group has yet to emerge in response to the ongoing federal investigation into whether the 40-year-old former NBA [National Basketball Association] referee made calls to manipulate point totals and conspired with gamblers who had ties to organized crime. Rep. Bobby Rush of Illinois, the chairman of the House Sub-committee on Commerce, Trade and Consumer Protection, wrote to NBA commissioner David Stern last week [in late July 2007], "If the allegations prove true, this could be one of the most damaging scandals in the history of American sports." But there are most assuredly dissenting opinions about the third prong of the sports world's ongoing misadventures—the pursuit by presumed steroid cheat Barry Bonds of Hank Aaron's hallowed home run record, which Bonds remained one short of matching through Monday night. [Bonds hit his 756th home run on August 8, 2007, to break Aaron's career record.]

Media Feasts

As the sports media spare no saliva in covering these events—ESPN blanketed the Vick hearing with a blessed armada that

---

1. As of [September] 2009, Michael Vick [had returned to the NFL, having completed part of] a . . . federal sentence on felony charges related to dogfighting. In November of 2008, Vick received a three-year suspended state (Virginia) sentence for dogfighting under terms of a plea bargain that also includes a $2,500 fine and four years' probation.

included the *NFL* [National Football League] *Live* crew, the Outside the Lines crew and the legal analysis crew—a search for perspective becomes almost as imperative as the search for truth and justice. In the 24/7 news cycle that holds sway over us, misbehaving athletes and misbehaving referees sometimes get way too much coverage (something they share with freeway car chases and the after-hours antics of tabloid party queens), and so the wheel of public opinion takes a reverse spin.

Vick, accused on July 17[, 2007,] in an 18-page indictment of sponsoring and wagering on dogfighting and of treating his dogs with chilling cruelty, becomes, in more and more circles, the one who is being wronged. A plane flies over the Falcons' training camp in Flowery Branch, Ga., last Thursday pulling a banner that reads, NEW TEAM NAME? DOG-KILLERS?, and tight end Alge Crumpler says hopefully, "I was wondering when it was going to run out of gas." Denver Nuggets guard Allen Iverson, no stranger to run-ins with the law and, like Vick, a native of southeastern Virginia, tells Vick to "keep his head up" and suggests that he is being pursued by authorities because there is always a "bull's-eye" on prominent athletes. Former Atlanta coach Dan Reeves says that he would "do anything I could to help Mike."

And while Dodson was the only person in a number 7 [jersey] spotted inside the courtroom, several more so attired held a Vick vigil outside the building. "It was time that someone should step up and support him," said Nick Fontecchio, who with two friends made the nine-hour drive from Boston to stand by their man. Michael Geary, one of Fontecchio's pals, called Vick "the most exciting player in football" and observed that "you never know what he's going to do next." (Insert joke here.) Perhaps this should be viewed as a Kumbaya moment for America: Caucasians from a city known for racial tension heading south in support of an African-American.

We've seen a similar shift regarding Bonds, who hit home run number 754 last Friday night [July 27, 2007]. The fact that the 43-year-old San Francisco Giants slugger is skewered in the media is the very reason to embrace him more tightly. For the fans at AT&T Park and the paddlers in McCovey Cove last week, the hovering media pack is as welcome as an invasion of killer bees. The mood at the ballpark can be characterized thusly: Fans just want to be in attendance when Bonds breaks the record, the Giants just want Bonds to break the record so the media will leave them alone, and opponents just want Bonds to break the record because they are sick to death of having to answer questions about a controversy that doesn't concern them.

Legal and Business Issues

Last week the spotlight fell most harshly on Vick. On Monday, four days after Vick said in a statement that he "looks forward to clearing my good name," a codefendant in the case, Tony Taylor, changed his plea to guilty and signed a statement in which he said that Vick supplied almost all of the money used to run the dogfighting operation and to bet on fights. Taylor said he was not promised a lighter sentence by prosecutors, but he is now expected to testify against Vick and the two other defendants, Purnell Peace and Quanis Phillips. The four men were partners in Bad Newz Kennels, which operated on a property owned by Vick in Surry County, Va., but Taylor was reportedly not as close to Vick as the other codefendants and recently was not as involved in the kennel's business.

The developments only deepened the perception that Vick's chances of playing in 2007 are slim, and not just because NFL commissioner Roger Goodell barred him from attending training camp. The animal-rights groups that have demonstrated outside the Falcons' gates represent a powerful lobby—it's as if the Vick case was the one they were waiting for. An official from the Humane Society told *SI* [*Sports Illustrated*] that the server that handles the organization's online donations crashed after the indictment was released, so vehement was the response to the graphic accusations it contained.

Businesses may put up with controversial behavior, but only until it affects the bottom line.

Plus, Judge Henry E. Hudson has scheduled the trial to start on Nov. 26, making it unlikely that the Falcons would hand an undeniably talented but scatter-armed quarterback the ball just to have him hand it back late in the season as he assumed the lead role in another edition of must-see Court TV. Taking the long view, if Vick is convicted—the maximum punishment for the charges against him is five years in prison and fines of up to $250,000—Goodell's decision on the QB's future playing status will be easy. But if Billy Martin, Vick's celebrity attorney who has represented Monica Lewinsky and former NBA forward Jayson Williams, arranges a plea that keeps him out of prison, Goodell's choice becomes much more difficult.

Some of the NFL's corporate partners have already spoken. Last week Nike suspended its lucrative deal with Vick, Reebok announced that it would stop selling his jersey, and two trading card companies (Donruss and Upper Deck) said that his card will no longer be part of their 2007 sets. Vick's fate with Donruss was hardly surprising: Ann Powell, the president of the company, comes to work each day in Arlington, Texas, accompanied by her five dogs, who have the run of the office. Says a Reebok spokesperson, "The number of e-mails and statements we're getting from consumers was pretty telling about how disturbing people find these allegations to be." Reebok does not have a business relationship with Vick but is the NFL's official uniform supplier.

That is the Don Imus [American radio host noted for scandalous comments] principle at work: Businesses may put up with controversial behavior, but only until it affects the bottom line.

Race May Play a Role

No one has yet come out and said that Vick is being prosecuted because he's black, but reporters who have ventured into Vick's hometown of Newport News, Va., find almost unanimous support for him among African-American residents. No doubt they identify with him as a native son; perhaps they are also more acutely aware of instances of racial discrimination in the criminal justice system. The Virginians cite Vick's donations of school supplies, athletic uniforms and air conditioners to the underprivileged. "There should be more role models like him," a woman named Misha Brown told the Associated Press.

The noted newspaper pundit Deion Sanders came close to excusing Vick in a July 22 [2007] column in *The News-Press* of Fort Myers, Fla., seemingly referencing his own black, Southern roots. "Some people enjoy proving they have the biggest, toughest dog on the street," wrote Sanders, the former NFL and MLB [Major League Baseball] star who is now an analyst for NFL Network. "I bet Vick loves the dogs that were the biggest and the baddest. Maybe he identified with them in some way. You can still choose to condemn him, but I'm trying to take you inside his mind so you can understand where he might be coming from." Sanders also echoed sentiments previously expressed by former Dallas Cowboys running back Emmitt Smith that Vick is being persecuted because of his fame while the ringleaders in the dogfighting business go unpursued. "The only thing I can gather from this situation is that we're using Vick," wrote Sanders.

Race is an issue as well with Bonds, who is the subject of an ongoing federal grand-jury investigation into perjury and tax-evasion charges. Polls consistently show that black baseball fans are more likely than white fans by more than two to one to look favorably on Bonds's quest for 756 and much more likely to think he has been treated unfairly by the media. The Donaghy matter didn't have obvious racial overtones, though comedian Lewis Black did note on *The Daily Show* ... "Whoever thought it would be a white guy who would mess up the NBA?"

"We throw around words like decay and deteriorate, but there are more people watching, listening and logging on to sports than ever in history."

But the mere mention of race and steroids and indictments and gambling was enough to sour the stomach of many American sports fans on these hot summer days—especially that of baseball superfan Bud Selig. Still, the commissioner finally announced on July 24 [2007] that he would attend San Francisco's games until Bonds broke Aaron's record—except for last weekend, when he was in Cooperstown for the Hall of Fame induction ceremonies. Fortunately (or unfortunately, depending on your perspective), Bonds failed to homer on Saturday or Sunday, giving Selig the opportunity to rejoin the Giants for their road swing through Los Angeles and San Diego.

Fan Interest Continues

Looking at the big picture, at a time when American soldiers are dying daily in a godforsaken civil war thousands of miles away, well, perhaps it is time to turn down the volume on Vick, Bonds and Donaghy. "If you look at each of these things carefully, you realize that they are not going to have any measurable impact on the public's affection for and allegiance to those major sports," says Neal Pilson, the former president of CBS Sports who now runs a sports consulting business. "We throw around words like decay and deteriorate, but there are more people watching, listening and logging on to sports than ever in history."

Fair enough. But let's also remember that there have to be many sets of eyes on our games (and, obviously, not just referees' eyes) to assure us that they are not degraded by bad people doing bad things. Addressing the National Association of Sports Officials at its 25th annual convention in Denver on Sunday, founder and president Barry Mano reached back to 17th-century Spanish philosopher Baltasar Gracian to find a suitable way to frame the issues of the day. "One breath of scandal," Mano said, "freezes much honorable sweat."

5

Team-Sport Athletes Are Encouraged to Be Poor Role Models

Ian Warden

Ian Warden is a reporter and feature writer for The Canberra Times, *one of Australia's leading newspapers.*

Recent psychological studies have indicated that team-sport members display an alarming absence of morality and sense of responsibility toward, and respect for, others. Attributing factors for this phenomenon among athletes include lowered educational demands, lack of moral guidance and consequences for poor behavior, "group mentality," and general apathy among the media and fans—who are mostly concerned with seeing their teams emerge victorious. Whereas individual sports, such as golf and tennis, generally hold their participants to high moral standards, the roughness of team play, so encouraged and applauded on the field, all too often transcends the final whistle.

A mong athletes why is the off-field behaviour of footballers so spectacularly awful? Why can't footballers be more like tennis players? At this year's [2007] Wimbledon [tennis tournament] . . . as usual there doesn't seem to have been a single off-court instance of wee-small-hours drinking, drug-taking, buttock-baring or punch-throwing among the competitors.

Is there something about football and footballers?

United States sports ethicist Professor Sharon K. Stoll (she rejoices in the title of director of the University of Idaho's

Ian Warden, "When Footie Stars Snap," *The Canberra Times*, July 26, 2007. Copyright © 2007, Rural Press Limited. Reproduced by permission of the author.

Centre for Ethical Theory and Honour in Competition and Sport) thinks that, yes, there is something. She's examined the capacity for "moral reasoning" among 72,000 athletes and found male footballers along with male ice-hockey and lacrosse players have the poorest "moral reasoning" abilities of all athletes. Golfers and tennis players have much better moral-reasoning skills and non-athletes are more moral still. More of Stoll and her enormous (and growing) sample of tens of thousands of the sporting kind in a moment.

Meanwhile, as an AAP [Australian Associated Press] news story summed it up recently, "The football season is only at the halfway point but already Australia's leather-chasing heroes have compiled a huge off-field shame file. Assaults, sexual indiscretions, [drunk driving], nightclub fist fights, street brawls: the catalogue stretches across the four football codes, with rugby league and AFL [Australian Football League] Australian rules players easily the worst offenders." As well as the [rugby player] Todd Carney imbroglio of such special interest to Canberrans, there has been the example of the [rugby team] Fremantle Dockers' Chris Tarrant baring his celebrity buttocks in a Darwin nightspot and then punching someone with one of his famous fists.

Journalists and lay citizens tend not to analyse footballers' behaviour and to just deplore it and scoff at it (one ABC [Australian Broadcasting Corp.] Radio National wit, commenting on [rugby player] Lote Tuquiri's latest brush with the demon drink, called him "Lote Daiquiri").

Sports Mentality Discourages Morality

Stoll, though, sounded as if she might have a scholarly overview of the issue. I sent her some news reports of recent shocks and horrors among our leather-chasing heroes, but of course the US has a plethora of these sorts of things among its own sporting millionaires with Year 10 educations.

She's been studying morality in sports since the 1980s and she measures what she calls moral reasoning by asking student athletes to make written responses to various competitive sporting and commonplace life scenarios she's composed in which there's always a stupid, violent or cheating and Machiavellian [greedy] option. She measures how athletes think about the issues of morality as applied to sport and she comes across startling amounts of moral illiteracy.

Her research shows, she says, that athletes have worse moral-reasoning skills than non-athletes. Male team sport athletes such as footballers are the worst. Male athletes who compete for money are more morally illiterate than male amateur athletes.

"When you're allowed to hit someone within the rules, you start to view your opponent as an object and not human."

All female athletes, professional or amateur, score better than all male athletes at moral reasoning, but the women's ethical standards are withering apace so that the professor expects their scores to be as awful as men's within five years. And all morally illiterate athletes can, she finds, be taught to be moral as long as there are timely, painstakingly devised moral educational "interventions". She thinks immoral athletes reflect in part their immoral times. She says, "I'm not sure that young people today really do know what's right ... and how to make a reasoned response and I'm not so sure they have a clue as to what a moral issue is or why it's important in their lives. We live in difficult times when most of us aren't quite sure what is right and wrong."

Loss of Respect for Others

And so she thinks athletes need "an intervention" like a course she's devised called Winning With Character. It's meant to teach coaches how to teach their athletes (in a 20- to 30-minute class once a week for the academic year) to show some character, which for Stoll, boils down to the Dalai Lamaesque [after the Tibetan Buddhist leader] credo of "having a strong knowledge and awareness of other people."

Alas, achieving this is an uphill struggle, especially with players of the biffing, crunching, body-contact sports, because, "When you're allowed to hit someone within the rules, you start to view your opponent as an object and not human."

I lobbed her various devil's advocacy questions, most of which she smashed away with aplomb.

The off-field behaviour of footballers seems so awful that I wondered if perhaps they were a kind of ugly, gladiatorial breed and beyond the reach of moral teaching?

And are they really "role models"? The way they play their sports is so physical, so reckless that perhaps those of us who love to watch their sports (especially slightly built, physically timid people like this writer) even half-enjoy the fact that so many of them seem to come from a kind of dangerous underclass? Can thrilling football be played by moral men?

But Stoll doesn't agree that footballers are an underclass beyond morals. What's wrong, she thinks, is that adored, fabulously paid male athletes like footballers have got "away with being special all of their lives, and few times have had to pay the consequences."

The essence of a sport somehow resides in the character of those who play it.

"They're no different than you or I . . . except that they've been made to feel special from day one. If you read about moral development you'll know that their perspective is the direct result of little or no consequences, little moral education, and poor role models."

Morality Must Be Taught

Her programs of educational "interventions" are especially aimed at coaches since they are so often the immediate role models of morally challenged athletes. It's entertaining to imagine hardened, ruthless Australian football coaches taking her *Winning With Character* course. She's a Christian but doesn't think that's why she's so preoccupied with sports sinners. "I was raised in a Christian family and had aspirations of being a pastor. However, moral education is not framed by any one religion. All the world's nine great religions argue for a moral direction and one could be an atheist and still believe in morality and moral education."

And, yes, she's adamant, these bad boys are role models in that "anyone who is selling a product, whether it is a spectator sport or an entertainment, these individuals are role models whether they like it or not" because the essence of a sport somehow resides in the character of those who play it.

She smashes away my feeble lob of the idea of footballers being from a gladiatorial underclass from which we mustn't, morally, expect too much.

"Morality isn't somehow bred in the upper classes, leaving all the lower classes as immoral little whatevers. Morality doesn't somehow limit itself to one group or another, or one race, or one gender. Morality is the basic and decent way in which we are expected to treat each other and how we live our lives.

"I'm often asked about moral absolutes[.] I like to quote [author] Christina Hoff Sommers who wrote an important piece in which she said, 'Do absolutes exist?' She said, 'Yes they do[. I]t is absolutely wrong to rape. It is absolutely wrong to abuse children and it is absolutely right to love.' So if these absolutes exist, then we need to rethink the notion that no absolutes exist. Athletes need to also consider the same."

Team Sports Encourage Tribe Mentality

I wondered why tennis players behave so much better than footballers and, in her findings, think so much more morally? Stoll thinks that as well as the important basic facts of tennis not (usually) being a team sport with a tribe mentality and not being a sport where biffing, hurting and loathing is required there's the eerily, indefinably important fact that children who play tennis begin with the expectation that they have some ethical, moral obligations to others when they're playing, the most obvious being the need to, fairly, call opponents' balls in or out. And so, for her, tennis, like golf in which, again, the individual player has several obligations to be truthful "has a different culture and tradition."

"Moral reasoning is a systematic and intentional activity that is affected by discussion, reflection, thought, reading, culture, and tradition. Tennis and golf meet many of these criteria [but] most team sports don't meet any of them."

Yes, I remember one aghast journalistic colleague at one Australian Open [tennis tournament] being told to follow-up her idiot editor's bright idea that, surely, with 300 of the world's sexiest and most hormone-propelled young people (the tennis players) unleashed in Melbourne there must be some great shock, horror, outrage stories to find about their various all-night debaucheries together. Tennis players just aren't like that, she pleaded, correctly, but still had to go through the pointless motions of calling around, of course in vain, the city's fleshpots to ask if they ever saw any tennis celebrity buttock-baring and brawling.

6

Overly Demonstrative Black Athletes Set a Bad Example

Thad Mumford

Thad Mumford, a former New York Yankee batboy, is a sports columnist for the New York Times.

In earlier times, when a football player scored a touchdown, he handed or tossed the ball to the referee and modestly accepted some congratulations from his teammates while jogging back to the sidelines. Today's leaping reception or bull-dozing run is often celebrated with loud, boisterous self-congratulation, camera-mugging and exaggerated physical hijinks reminiscent of vaude-villian acts wherein the black characters were often cast in a court-jester light. The modern-day player still recognizes the brilliantly painted goal line; however, the line between freedom of expression and ridiculous behavior has become increasingly blurred.

There has never been a better time to be a black athlete. Moneywise, it is now a sum-of-zeros game. (If only my parents had seen the long-term value of studying Rod Carew's books on hitting instead of math and chemistry.) African-Americans have turned white football and basketball players into tokens. And while our representation in baseball continues its decline, the percentage of blacks who dominate the game continues to surge. The reign of Tiger Woods and the

Williams sisters could lead to a time when country club athletic equipment will be on back order in Harlem's sporting goods stores.

Advertisers now line up to have black sports figures push their products, especially to the audience they covet, with near-liturgical zeal, 18- to 25-year-old white suburban males, many of whom are mesmerized by the idiomatic hip-hop jargon, the cock-of-the-walk swagger, the smooth-as-the-law-allows attire of their black heroes.

But there is a downside to all this. The unsayable but unassailable truth is that the clowning, dancing, preening smack-talker is becoming the Rorschach image of the African-American male athlete. It casts a huge shadow over all other images. This persona has the power to sell what no one should buy: the notion that black folks are still cuttin' up for the white man.

Any ethnic group that ever found itself on the periphery of equality and acceptance has had to create coping mechanisms. Some who were victimized by bigotry secretly mimicked the prejudicial perceptions of their oppressor with exaggerated, self-deprecating depictions of their behaviour, their very private burlesque that gave them brief respites from their marginalization.

For African-Americans, burlesque as healing balm became the essential comedic ingredient of black vaudeville. Comics would strut and cakewalk through now classic routines that savagely lampooned minstrel shows, popular staples of mainstream vaudeville in which white performers in blackface and coily-haired wigs further dehumanized their own creation, the darkie prototype.

Black vaudeville would become a casualty of expanding educational opportunities that created an evolving black middle class with deep concerns that minstrel-like characterizations were degrading and would only perpetuate the accepted attitude that the Negro was the slap-happy court jester for whites.

But a variety of factors, in particular the canonizing of youth culture, the de-emphasizing of wisdom and the glorification of the boorishness inherent in America's look-at-me culture, has played a major role in putting black vaudeville back on the boards. The featured attraction? A number of black athletes.

When we see a wide receiver strut and cakewalk to the end zone, then join teammates in the catalog of celebratory rituals, which now feature props, or hear a cackling, bug-eyed commentator speaking Slanglish ("Give up the props, dog, they be flossin' now!"), we are seeing our private burlesque, out of context, without its knowing wink and satiric spine. Minus these elements, what remains is minstrel template made ubiquitous by Stepin Fetchit and the handful of black actors who worked in the early motion pictures.

But the athletes who have exhumed the minstrel's grave keep alive these shopworn condescensions.

But unlike the Stepin Fetchits, left with no alternative but to mortgage their dignity for a paycheck, who often suffered tremendously under the weight of tremendous guilt and shame, some of today's black athletes have unwittingly packaged and sold this nouveau minstrel to Madison Avenue's highest bidders, selling it as our "culturally authentic" behaviour, "keepin' it real," as they say.

Nothing could be less real or more inauthentic. Or condescending. How can 38 million people possibly have a single view of reality or authenticity? But the athletes who have exhumed the minstrel's grave keep alive these shopworn condescensions.

"The danger of the domination of these one-dimensional images is that they deny the humanity and the intellectuality of an entire people, eliminating the possibility of them being taken seriously," said Harry Edwards, a professor of sociology at San Jose State who is a consultant to the National Football League.

White adults, whose knowledge of black life is generally limited to what they see in pop culture, take burlesque at face value. This reinforces what was considered culturally authentic, that black people are funny as all get-out.

We now allow people to take the pride and dignity from our athletes by celebrating them when they play for the camera.

But the athletes aren't the main culprits. That, of course, would be television, which has brought its two major contributions to American culture, sex and excess, to every sport. TV has erased the line that separated sports from entertainment and created a product that encourages the marketing of black burlesque. Call it athle-tainment.

"We now allow people to take the pride and dignity from our athletes by celebrating them when they play for the camera," said Al Downing, a veteran of 15 major league seasons, now doing public relations for the Los Angeles Dodgers.

It can be a dizzying ride. Today's African-American athletes have been handled like porcelain eggs from the moment it became clear that preparing for the next game was of greater significance than preparing for the SAT. Then once they become seven- and eight-figure Hessians, they are walled off from the real world, and all accountability, by management, agents and corporate sponsors, who are all blessed with fertile amounts of unctuousness ("You rule, bro!"). The word "no" has become a museum piece. As football Hall of Famer Deacon Jones once said, "There's no school that teaches you how to be a millionaire." But does this mean that athletes who feel the need to pay homage to every tackle with a dance step, who triumphantly crow in the face of opponents after monster dunks, should be excused for not knowing the line between exuberance and bad sportsmanship?

Those most vulnerable to this confusion are the children, far too many growing up with mangled notions of race, manhood and sports.

"I'm more impressed by someone like a Barry Sanders, athletes who do their jobs without having to show up the opposition," said Bill White, whose major-league career spanned 13 years.

Issues of cultural identity are complicated, contradictory and complex. One person's ethnic burlesque is another's sense of cultural autonomy. Questions beget more questions. If we keep our burlesque private, are we capitulating to people who feel we should be ashamed of this behaviour? Aren't there more appropriate times and places to have fun with our own stereotypes? But does regulating this behaviour inadvertently marginalize those African-Americans trapped in burlesquelike worlds? Is there a possible connection between the actions of the white fan who cheers rabidly after sack dances on Sunday, then may be reluctant to grant bank loans for black businesses on Monday?

Those most vulnerable to this confusion are the children, far too many growing up with mangled notions of race, manhood and sports. Black athletes who take our burlesque public could tell them, in the lingua-slanga they share, that there is a difference between having style and actin' the fool. Or that reading and speaking proper English isn't a punk white-boy thing. Or that their chances of playing professional sports are extremely remote. So, if these children do have athletic ability, they should think of using it for one purpose to get a free education.

7

Sportsfans Are Responsible for Steroid Use Among Professional Athletes

Chuck Klosterman

Chuck Klosterman has written for publications including GQ, Esquire, the New York Times Magazine, and the Washington Post. His articles mainly encompass pop culture and sports, and he has become a regular contributor to ESPN The Magazine's "Page Two." In addition, he has written five books.

Although performance-enhancing substances have apparently been used among athletes for decades, today's clamor for ever-more exciting, faster competition has resulted in a high rate of usage, particularly among pro football players. In a violent game where size and speed play a greater role than in any other, it is not surprising that participants seek an artificial physical edge in order to remain competitive. While there is continuing controversy about whether record-setting statistics are compromised by substance use, the rise in popularity and interest whenever a long-held record is broken suggests that, at least according to profit and popularity standards, the demand for statistical results far outweighs the suggestion of unethical advantage gained by substance use. Furthermore, despite their proven inherent future physiological danger, players will continue to use and abuse the performance-enhancers so long as the general public continues the applause and encouragement.

Chuck Klosterman, "Why We Look the Other Way," *ESPN.com*, March 26, 2007. © 2007 ESPN/Starwave Partners d/b/a ESPN Internet Venture. Reprinted courtesy of ESPN.com.

Shawne Merriman weighs 272 pounds.

This is six pounds less than Anthony Muñoz, probably the most dominating left tackle of all time. Shawne Merriman also runs the 40-yard dash in 4.61 seconds. When Jerry Rice attended the NFL draft combine in 1985, he reportedly ran a 4.60; Rice would go on to gain more than 23,000 all-purpose yards while scoring 207 career touchdowns.

You do not need Mel Kiper's hard drive to deduce what these numbers mean: As an outside linebacker, Shawne Merriman is almost as big as the best offensive tackle who ever played and almost as fast as the best wide receiver who ever played. He is a rhinoceros who moves like a deer. Common sense suggests this combination should not be possible. It isn't.

Merriman was suspended from the San Diego Chargers for four games last season after testing positive for the anabolic steroid nandrolone. He argues this was the accidental result of a tainted nutritional supplement. "I think two out of 10 people will always believe I did something intentional, or still think I'm doing something," Merriman has said. If this is truly what he believes, no one will ever accuse him of pragmatism. Virtually everyone who follows football assumes Merriman used drugs to turn himself into the kind of hitting machine who can miss four games and still lead the league with 17 sacks. He has been caught and penalized, and the public shall forever remain incredulous of who he is and what he does.

Within the context of any given game, nobody cares how a certain linebacker got so big while remaining so fast.

The public knows the truth, or at least part of it. And knowing this partial truth, the public will return to ignoring this conundrum almost entirely.

The public will respond by renewing its subscription to *NFL Sunday Ticket*, where it will regularly watch dozens of 272-pound men accelerate at speeds that would have made them Olympic sprinters during the 1960s. This, it seems, is the contemporary relationship most people have with drugs and pro football: unconditional distrust of anyone who tests positive, balanced by an unconscious willingness to overlook all the physical impossibilities they see. This is partially understandable; socially, sports serve an escapist purpose. Football players are real people, but they exist in a constructed nonreality. Within the context of any given game, nobody cares how a certain linebacker got so big while remaining so fast. Part of what makes football successful is its detachment from day-to-day life. For 60 minutes, it subsists in a vacuum. But this detachment is going to become more complicated in the coming years, mostly because reality is evolving, becoming harder to block out. And the Evolved Reality is this: It's starting to feel like a significant segment of the NFL is on drugs.

As a consequence, you will have to make some decisions.

Not commissioner Roger Goodell.

You.

On Feb. 27, federal, state and local authorities seized the records of an Orlando pharmacy, accusing the owners of running an online bazaar for performance-enhancing drugs. This came on the heels of a raid on a similar enterprise in Mobile, Ala., where the customer list apparently included recognizable names like boxer Evander Holyfield and late-blooming outfielder Gary Matthews Jr.

None of this is particularly shocking.

But then there is the case of Richard Rydze. In 2006 Rydze, an internist, purchased $150,000 of testosterone and human growth hormone from the Florida pharmacy over the Internet. This is not against the law. However, Rydze is a physician for the Pittsburgh Steelers. He says he never prescribed any of those drugs to members of the team, and I cannot prove otherwise. However, the Steelers have had a complicated relationship with performance enhancers for a long time. Offensive lineman Steve Courson (now deceased) admitted he used steroids while playing for Pittsburgh in the 1970s and early '80s, as did at least four other guys. Former Saints coach Jim Haslett, a player in Buffalo from 1979 to 1985, has said the old Steelers dynasty essentially ran on steroids. The team, obviously, denies this.

That's what people want in a football player—someone who's crazy and mean.

Several members of the Carolina Panthers' 2004 Super Bowl team were implicated in a steroid scandal involving Dr. James Shortt, a private practitioner in West Columbia, S.C. One of these players was punter Todd Sauerbrun. Do not mitigate the significance of this point: *The punter was taking steroids.* The punter had obtained syringes and injectable Stanozolol, the same chemical Ben Johnson used before the 1988 Olympics. I'm not suggesting punters aren't athletes, nor am I overlooking how competitive the occupation of punting must be; I'm merely pointing out that it's kind of crazy to think punters would be taking steroids but defensive tackles would not. We all concede that steroids, HGH and blood doping can help people ride bicycles faster through the Alps. Why do we even momentarily question how much impact they must have on a game built entirely on explosion and power?

"People may give a certain amount of slack to football players because there's this unspoken sense that in order to play the game well, you need an edge," USC critical studies professor Todd Boyd told the Los Angeles Times last month. Boyd has written several books about sports, race and culture. "That's what people want in a football player—someone who's crazy and mean."

It's a subtle paradox: People choose to ignore the relationship between performance enhancers and the NFL because it's unquestionably the league where performance enhancers would have the biggest upside. But what will happen when such deliberate naïveté becomes impossible? Revelatory drug scandals tend to escalate exponentially (look at Major League Baseball and U.S. track and field). Merriman, Sauerbrun and the other 33 players suspended by the NFL since 2002 could be exceptions; it seems far more plausible they are not. We are likely on the precipice of a bubble that is going to burst. But if it does, how are we supposed to feel about it? Does this invalidate the entire sport, or does it barely matter at all?

This is where things become complicated.

It can be strongly argued that the most important date in the history of rock music was Aug. 28, 1964. This was the day Bob Dylan met the Beatles in New York City's Hotel Delmonico and got them high.

Obviously, a lot of people might want to disagree with this assertion, but the artistic evidence is hard to ignore. The introduction of marijuana altered the trajectory of the Beatles' songwriting, reconstructed their consciousness and prompted them to make the most influential rock albums of all time. After the summer of 1964, the Beatles started taking serious drugs, and those drugs altered their musical performance. Though it may not have been their overt intent, the Beatles took performance-enhancing drugs. And this is germane to sports for one reason: Absolutely no one holds it against them. No one views *Rubber Soul* and *Revolver* as "less authentic" albums, despite the fact that they would not (and probably could not) have been made by people who weren't on drugs.

Jack Kerouac wrote *On the Road* on a Benzedrine binge, yet nobody thinks this makes his novel less significant. A Wall Street stockbroker can get jacked up on cocaine before going into the trading pit, yet nobody questions his bottom line. It's entirely possible that you take 10mg of Ambien the night before a big day at the office, and then drink 32 ounces of coffee when you wake up (possibly along with a mind-sharpening cigarette). Anytime a person takes drugs for purposes that aren't exclusively recreational (i.e., staring at your stereo speakers, watching *Planet of the Apes*, etc.), he or she is using them to do something at a higher level. Yes, I realize there is a difference between caffeine and HGH. But there's probably an even greater difference between a morning of data processing and trying to cut-block Shawne Merriman.

My point is not that all drugs are the same, nor that drugs are awesome, nor that the Beatles needed LSD to become the geniuses they already were. My point is that sports are unique in the way they're retrospectively colored by the specter of drug use. East Germany was an Olympic force during the 1970s and '80s; today, you can't mention the East Germans' dominance without noting that they were pumped full of Ivan Drago-esque chemicals. This relationship changes the meaning of their achievements. You simply don't see this in other idioms. Nobody looks back at Pink Floyd's *Dark Side of the Moon* and says, "I guess that music is okay, but it doesn't really count. Those guys were probably high in the studio."

Now, the easy rebuttal to this argument is contextual, because it's not as if Roger Waters was shooting up with testosterone in order to strum his bass-guitar strings *harder*. Unlike songwriting or stock trading, football is mostly physical; it seems like there needs to be a different scale—an uncrossable line—for what endangers competitive integrity. But how do we make that distinction? In all of these cases (sports-related and otherwise), people are putting foreign substances into their bodies in the hope of reaching a desired result. The motive is the same. What's different, and sometimes arbitrary, is when people care. Baseball fans are outraged that Rafael Palmeiro tested positive for Stanozolol; they are indifferent to the fact that most players regularly took amphetamines for 40 years. Meanwhile, as a member of the Philadelphia Eagles in

1994, Bill Romanowski electively received two trauma IVs to help recover from injuries. Trauma IVs are what emergency room doctors give to people dying from car accidents. In his autobiography, Romanowski claims one of his teammates received six trauma IVs in the span of one season. This is natural?

For the sake of entertainment, we expect these people to be the fastest, strongest, most aggressive on earth.

I am told we live in a violent society. But even within that society, football players are singular. Another former Eagle, strong safety Andre Waters, committed suicide last November at age 44. A postmortem examination of his brain indicated he had the neurological tissue of an 85-year-old man with Alzheimer's, almost certainly the result of using his skull as a weapon for 12 seasons. Andre Waters hit people so hard, and so often, that he cut his time on earth in half. Hitting was his life. This is why the relationship between drugs and football is different from the relationship between drugs and baseball: Baseball is mostly about tangible statistics, which drugs skew and invalidate; football is more about intangible masculine warfare, which drugs quietly enhance.

Announcers casually lionize pro football players as gladiators, but that description is more accurate than most would like to admit. For the sake of entertainment, we expect these people to be the fastest, strongest, most aggressive on earth. If they are not, they make less money and eventually lose their jobs.

This being the case, it seems hypocritical to blame them for taking steroids. We might blame them more if they did not.

Around this time last year, I wrote an essay for *The Magazine* about Barry Bonds—specifically, how steroids made his passing of Babe Ruth on the career home run list problematic.

I still believe this to be true, just as I believe that the notion of an NFL that's more juiced than organic is more negative than interesting. It would be easier to be a football fan if none of this was going on. But since it is going on, we will all have to decide how much this Evolved Reality is going to bother us.

On Sunday, we have wanted them to be superfast, super-strong, superentertaining, and, weirdly, superethical.

This will not be simple. I don't think there will be a fall guy for the NFL; over time, we won't be able to separate Merriman from the rest of the puzzle (which MLB has so far successfully done with Bonds). It won't be about the legitimacy of specific players. This will be more of an across-the-board dilemma, because we will have to publicly acknowledge that the most popular sport in the country has been kinetically altered by drugs, probably for the past 25 years. In many ways, the NFL's reaction barely matters. What matters more is how fans will attempt to reconcile that realization with their personal feelings toward the game. The question, ultimately, is this: If it turns out the lifeblood of the NFL is unnatural, does that make the game less meaningful?

The answer depends on who you are. And maybe how old you are.

In 1982, I read a story about Herschel Walker in *Sports Illustrated* headlined "My Body's Like an Army." It explained how, at the time, Walker didn't even lift weights; instead, he did 100,000 sit-ups and 100,000 push-ups a year, knocking out 25 of each every time a commercial came on the television. This information made me worship Herschel; it made him seem human and superhuman at the same time. "My Body's Like an Army" simultaneously indicated that I could become Herschel Walker and that I could never become Herschel Walker. His physical perfection was self-generated and completely pure. He had made himself better than other mortals, and that made me love him.

But I was 10 years old.

There comes a point in every normal person's life when they stop looking at athletes as models for living. Any thinking adult who follows pro sports understands that some people are corrupt and the games are just games and money drives everything. It would be strange if they did not realize these things. But what's equally strange is the way so many fans (and sportswriters, myself included) revert back to their 10-year-old selves whenever an issue like steroids shatters the surface.

Most of the time, we don't care what football players do when they're not playing football. On any given Wednesday, we have only a passing interest in who they are as people or how they choose to live. But Sunday is different. On Sunday, we have wanted them to be superfast, superstrong, superentertaining and, weirdly, superethical. They are supposed to be pristine 272-pound men who run 40 yards in 4.61 seconds simply because they do sit-ups during commercial breaks for "Grey's Anatomy." Unlike everybody else in America, they cannot do whatever it takes to succeed; they have to fulfill the unrealistic expectations of 10-year-old kids who read magazines. And this is because football players have a job that doesn't matter at all, except in those moments when it matters more than absolutely everything else.

It may be time to rethink some of this stuff.

8

Women in Traditionally Male Sports Do Not Need to Shed Their Femininity

Danica Patrick with Laura Morton

Danica Patrick, born March 25, 1982, in Beloit, Wisconsin, was the 2005 Indianapolis 500 Rookie of the Year and has since become the first female winner in IndyCar history, winning the 2008 Japan 500. Laura Morton is the author of 23 books and has written seven New York Times *bestsellers, including books with Melissa Etheridge, Joan Lunden, and Marilu Henner.*

Ever since she entered competition racing as a teenager, Danica Patrick, the highest qualifying and finishing female driver in the history of the Indy 500, has found herself under constant scrutiny. Her flashy temper has invited criticism and admiration among her male counterparts, but very few—if any—dare challenge her determination and commitment to the sport. In 2002, her decision to pose erotically in FHM *magazine created a whirlwind of controversy: can a female in a male-dominated sport demand equal treatment, and simultaneously use her gender as a publicity tool? Yes, she can be both: a competitive, hard-nosed and capable race car driver and a woman not ashamed to exploit her attractiveness and sexuality.*

A woman living in a man's world has been a recurring theme throughout my life. Having to prove myself over and over has become a part of my everyday living. It took me some time to understand and accept that there are benefits to being different. Once I did, I wanted to do everything I could to embrace it and capitalize on what made me special.

As much as I wanted to fit in, and as hard as I tried to be respected, I never seemed to penetrate that wall of male bonding or find acceptance from my peers. Even when I deserved to be commended or congratulated, I was never given the adulation I earned simply because I was a girl—which made me different, and in that respect kept me on the outside of the world of the men. Those years allowed me to focus on taking my differences and using them as an advantage. They helped me to find a sense of security within myself, because I was definitely not going to receive any kind of support from the outside.

Think about what kind of world this would be if we were all the same. If we all had the same things to offer, there would be no appreciation for the balance in the universe. Without bad days, you can't appreciate the good. Without defeat, you can't appreciate victory. Everybody has something they are really good at. You certainly have skills you can do as well as if not better than anyone else. There is something in your body, your mind, or your spirit that sets you apart that makes you different from the rest of the world. I was fortunate enough to find my something "different" when I was ten years old. Of course, I realize that doesn't happen for everyone, and that in itself is something that makes me different, because it happened to me.

Win with Confidence

There have been many times in my life when my attitude and level of self-assurance was the difference between winning and losing. Even when I don't win a race, I see victory in how I handle my losses or what I learned from the experience. Confidence and self-belief are like muscles that have to be built and used to be strong. My confidence has helped me to make smart choices and to keep cool along the way so that I never veered off course from my dream of becoming a professional driver. My courage keeps me driving with or without my confidence. There were a lot of opportunities for me to waver from the center of the road, but I had a bigger plan, a bigger strength, and that knowledge led me to never fall into situations of peer pressure or make choices that would ruin my career. The risk/reward ratio just never made sense in my life.

Racing is not about being masculine or feminine. It's about being a damn good driver.

It's been said that "ability without ambition is like kindling wood without a spark." Ambition is not a negative trait. It is an essential element to achieve success on any level. Any woman who becomes a leader in her workplace deals with the same kind of issues I face as the only woman competing for a win on the track. Jealousy, distrust, lack of approval from peers, doubt, and the constant need to demonstrate that you've earned your place in the company—they're all good excuses that work for a while, but if you're good at what you do, you'll make it.

Everybody is entitled to their own opinion. In the end their opinions don't mean a thing if your performance is superior. Those who talk negatively about other people are usually jealous, angry, threatened people. I've dealt with a lot of people questioning my performance as a driver—everyone from other team owners, drivers, journalists, and racing aficionados. I've been called dangerous, erratic, aggressive, and out of control. You know what? I don't care.

Racing is not about being masculine or feminine. It's about being a damn good driver. The track doesn't discriminate. Man or woman, you either have the skill or you don't. I find it's best to leave politics to the politicians. There's simply no room for excessive bullshit when your job is driving a racecar.

If I and my team, my pit crew, my engineer, my agent, my manager, or my sponsors are not all sharing the same goal, we are not working toward the same outcome, which, for me, is winning races. If we're not working with one another, then we are working against each other. That surely defeats the purpose of all being in business together. That lack of productivity means we are not winning races or living up to the obligations we all share as business associates. In any work environment, that has an impact of immeasurable proportion.

Respect Must Be Earned

I've learned that I don't need to be friends with the other drivers to compete, but I definitely want their acceptance and respect on the track. You get that only by earning it. It's not an automatic thing. If earning their respect makes me work harder, then I'm the one who reaps all the benefits. Telling myself I don't care about what other people think is one of the ways I have built my self-confidence over the years.

Tell yourself something long enough and sooner or later you'll start to believe it. Think of all of the ways your life will benefit by believing it doesn't matter what other people think. Confidence comes from within. It allows you to be comfortable and hold your head up in any situation. It's proving yourself over and over and over again, every time you face your toughest competition.

Confidence is when other people worry that you're in the game. It's walking right up to someone—anyone—shaking his hand hard, looking him right in the eyes, and talking to him face to face.

It's asking questions others wouldn't dare.

It's putting on a brave face even when you know there's a shadow of doubt or, for me, when I get nervous "butterfly" feelings in my stomach at the beginning of every race.

Everybody wants someone working for them with moxie, with confidence and courage. Confidence is expressive, but it should never be confused with being arrogant. It's shown by making eye contact with people when you talk to them. There's something about intense eye contact that gives you a connection with someone, if only for that moment. It lets him know you are present and care about what he is saying. It can convey that you are angry, attracted, joyful, sad, or aware.

A long time ago, I decided to never wear sunglasses when I am meeting someone for the first time. It's impersonal. My dad taught me to have a firm handshake—to "shake like you mean it." People have written about my handshake and how hard it is. I have made it a point to never let someone say I shake like a girl. I can look confident, feel confident, and be confident without ever saying a single word. It's a presence.

When I'm at the track I get a look of intense focus on my face. I call it my race face. I get a bit of a frown face on, and my eyes become squinty. People sometimes mistake this expression for being mad or upset—it is neither. I would rather look that way than any other way. Looking intense and focused is never wrong, and it can never be confused with looking arrogant, cocky, or over-confident.

Figuring out what makes you different in this world is one of the best ways to tap into your inner strengths. Find out what you're good at. If you're a fiery-tempered person, how can you use your aggression in a positive way? You surely won't be happy working in the local public library, but maybe you can tap that aggression and become a boxing coach or a salesperson? If you are an impatient person, waiting tables probably isn't your calling, but a job with instant gratification, like cutting hair, might be perfect for you. Try to use your differences to your advantage by putting yourself in situations that are beneficial to your skill set. . . .

Trying To Fit In

There were times when I hid being different, at least to the extent that I could. When I was in England, I deliberately lived like one of the guys in order to get along and to fit in. It was the only way I thought I could get through that painful and difficult phase of my life. I literally protected myself from being too girly. I was careful not to be too appealing or too feminine. I was closing myself off from being misunderstood or judged for wanting to be a racecar driver.

Running away from who I was meant I was living my life in a constant state of turmoil. Denying who you are or hiding behind some façade becomes like a cancer in your body that just spreads. Eventually it will manifest itself and take a toll on every aspect of your life. Living an inauthentic life holds you back from achieving your full potential.

It wasn't until I did a photo shoot for *FHM* magazine in 2002 that I had a full understanding that being a girl in a man's world wasn't a negative thing. That shoot changed a lot of people's perception of me—including my own. I thought it was pretty cool when I was asked to do a spread in their annual "Speed" section, a twenty-page layout dedicated to hot cars . . . and, I guess, me. I knew *FHM* wasn't putting a girl in the magazine who couldn't sell magazines or who didn't look pretty.

I had no idea what I would wear—a swimsuit, a race suit, or something totally different. I was tremendously flattered to be asked. It validated me in a way I had never known. Up to that point, every article I did, every magazine shoot, newspaper story, and television appearance focused on racing. *FHM* was different. It focused on my sexuality. For the first time in my life, I felt sexy, feminine, tough, and attractive all at the same time.

I worked hard at looking good in those photos. I worked out like a maniac and was so strict with my food. Let's just say that, like every thing else I do, I took this experience to the limit. I tried to tell myself that they wouldn't have to retouch a thing (they did—magazines retouch practically every photo you see). I no longer had a desire to hide being a woman from the world. In fact, I wanted to show it off—and I did—in every way, front, back, sitting, lying down. It was great fun.

Why not use whatever assets I have?

That spread forever eradicated having to answer for being "the girl" in racing, but it brought a whole new set of questions. Reporters went nuts wanting to know if I used my femininity to advance my career? How did I feel about becoming a sex symbol? It was crazy at first, but not long after the magazine was published I had an epiphany.

Why not?

Why not use whatever assets I have?

I'm confident in myself as a driver.

It's obvious I'm a girl, so why not use it as a tool?

There are benefits to it—benefits that I simply can't deny. People will doubt you, make you prove yourself over and over again, unlike a man might have to do. So what?

Here's the upshot. Sponsors such as Honda, Peak Antifreeze, and Secret deodorant have stepped up and are using a sexy woman race-car driver as a unique marketing tool. Let's face it, guys don't sell antifreeze quite the same way I do.

Everybody has assets they bring to any given situation. Learning to use them—better yet, learning not to be afraid to use them—is incredibly emancipating. It's taken me a long time, but I now know, without a doubt, that it's good to be a girl!

Though I wouldn't do it again, *FHM* gave people something to talk about. For the first time, people saw Danica Patrick as a woman first and a racer second. I had never known that kind of attention, and to be honest, it made me a little uncomfortable. I wouldn't change a thing about that experience. Because of it, I no longer need a sexy photo shoot to prove to the world that I'm a sexy woman. So if you're listening, [editor-in-chief] Anna Wintour, I am ready for *Vogue!*

That shoot helped me overcome my fears of others perceiving me as being too girly or out of place in the racing world. It helped me get sponsors because it generated a lot of attention. It was a risky decision on my part, but deep down I know the heightened awareness was a benefit. It got people talking. They are still talking and still running those photos. So was it worth it? You bet!

Be Who You Are

Being a girl is who I am, and that photo shoot opened the door for me to just be myself. As my confidence grew, so did my self-acceptance. Ultimately, I have learned that you've got to rock what you've got, whatever that is.

One of the benefits of being the only girl racing in the various series I have participated in is that I get to spend a lot of time around men, which has given me unusual perspective and insight into the way guys think. Women tend to over-rationalize, whereas men are very simple and obvious. No one edits themselves when I'm around, that's for sure. It's not like they curtail their conversations because there's a woman present. I hear firsthand what a guy is thinking when a pretty girl in a short skirt and high heels walks by. There were times in England when I found myself checking girls out with the guys, just to fit in. I'd ask, "Did you see that girl? She was hot!"

I think I have a pretty good understanding of the male psyche today as a result of my time spent being one of the boys. I think it has helped me in my relationship with [my husband] Paul. Most women spend a lot of time trying to figure out what their husbands or boyfriends are really thinking. I suppose I have the luxury of having spent so much time around men that I get it in a way most women simply can't. Come on, ladies . . . it's usually the most obvious answer, or they're just hungry!

I have wondered what it might be like if my husband were a professional racecar driver and someone I had to compete against. He's a very passionate guy, and he loves to win as much as I do. I'm guessing we'd be fierce competitors. Like me, Paul never quits. If he's competing, he wants to be the best. Since we share those qualities, we sometimes face each other in areas in which we both know we excel, yet one of us is slightly better than the other. Paul is such a good athlete; there's not much he can't do and do well. However, when it comes to yoga . . . well, let's just say I'm the one leading the class.

We try not to get into serious competition with each other because I know we're both very aware that we are serious competitors, and we could run with it to the point of creating unnecessary tension. So instead of trying to outdo each other, we have committed to accompanying each other. Whether it's cooking, running, hiking, or any other activity we do together, we try to complement each other and to work together on everything.

In any relationship, be it personal or professional, sharing the same goal and making the same commitment is the key to success. All relationships are never-ending learning experiences. Even relationships that don't work out teach us something of value. For me, my relationships prior to meeting my husband taught me various things I didn't want in a partner. Paul is the first man I have been with that I've had total confidence in knowing we are both in this relationship forever—and that I have his whole heart and he has mine. Our priorities are the same, and our commitment to live up to those priorities is unshakable. . . .

My presence in racing is making a difference. It is bringing on change.

I've never tried to be something that I'm not. I've just lived my life in a way in which I am frank, honest, and true to myself. In doing that, I don't have to change a thing about myself or the way I live. I don't have to do anything extra because I am out there giving a 100 percent effort each and every day. I just keep truckin' on, the same way I always have, because it works for me.

A Bigger Responsibility

There's a responsibility that comes with being a public personality. I have an obligation to live my life in [a] way that leads by example. I never gave much thought to the public part of being a racecar driver, but when I see young kids at a track wearing a T-shirt with my name on it or standing in line for an autograph at a race, I realize my life has influenced theirs. Recognizing that has helped me want to be a better role model to them.

I never had heroes growing up, just great role models. My parents were my best role models, giving me a strong set of values and teaching me to live responsibly. That knowledge has carried over into my adult life. I find myself having to make decisions about what I will endorse (watches, clothing, sunglasses) or won't (anything I don't believe in) or which photo shoots I will agree to (*Sports Illustrated*) and ones that I won't (*Playboy*). I have to factor in that I have a young fan base that looks up to me. It's a responsibility I am so flattered to have. It really humbles me. I'm so grateful for the opportunity to be a woman raising the bar for other girls—future champions coming up behind me, whether they are drivers, politicians, doctors, teachers, whatever they dream they can be. My presence in racing is making a difference. It is bringing on change. It is growing the sport and making people aware of the league.

I may not have been the first woman to race in the Indy 500, but it's a comfort to know that, because of all the women before me, I surely won't be the last.

All that makes me different in my life has made me unique and afforded me a tremendous opportunity to effect change.

So the next time someone points out something about you that makes you feel different, that makes you feel like an outsider, you tell them that all of those things are what makes you great—that being different means you're not like them—and that's all good.

Women Athletes Who Defy Cultural Traditions Cause Controversy

Umarah Jamali

Umarah Jamali is a writer based in New Delhi, India.

As the sporting world becomes more globalized and broadcast media extend their reach around the world, some countries are finding it difficult to balance newfound national pride in their athletes with a desire to hold on to longstanding traditions. Worldwide attention not only focuses on the athletes themselves, but also on the social mores and customs that can invite criticism and perhaps cast a darker shadow over already-tense relationships between people with differing religious or sociopolitical beliefs. This disparity is well illustrated by the case of a young female Muslim tennis star, whose prowess on the court warms some Indians even as it shames and infuriates others. The controversy has gained local, national, and even international attention.

Sania Mirza is having a great month [October 2005].

First, the fastest-rising player on the international tennis circuit (from No. 326 to as high as No. 31 in the past year)

Umarah Jamali, "Dressing Down a Role Model; Tennis pro Sania Mirza is adored in India, but her 'non-Islamic' outfits are another matter. Clerics issued a fatwa demanding she cover up," *The Globe and Mail* (Canada), October 22, 2005. Copyright © 2005 Globe Interactive, a division of Bell Globemedia Publishing, Inc. Reproduced by permission of the author.

was declared one of "Asia's heroes" in a special issue of *Time* that made her the first female Indian athlete ever featured on the magazine's cover.

Now, London's intellectual weekly *New Statesman* has listed the Mumbai-born 18-year-old as one of its "10 people capable of changing the world."

Calling the 5-foot-7 Ms. Mirza "the first significant female athlete of any kind in a country where women have been typically discouraged from taking up sport," the magazine says she has "the discipline, tenacity, flamboyance and, above all, the talent to ... inspire a whole new generation of Indian girls to express their hopes and ambitions through sport."

But will she be allowed to provide such inspiration?

It's true that an increasing number of Indian girls—especially Muslims—idolize Ms. Mirza.

Differing Views

Two weeks ago, the chairman of the board that administers 285 *madrassas* (Islamic schools) in the central state of Chhattisgarh announced that a new textbook for his more than 20,000 students would dedicate a chapter to her.

"She is representing the country and making India proud through her extraordinary talents," Adil Ahmed Khan explained. "She is the perfect role model for new-generation Muslims."

"We cannot consider her a good Muslim because she exposes her body in front of male spectators."

Many Muslim leaders congratulated him for the "encouraging" attempt to introduce the tennis icon to younger children, especially Muslim girls, who traditionally avoid sports.

But some clerics were outraged and launched a protest campaign, accusing Ms. Mirza of "defaming Islam by her non-Islamic way of playing the game"—a reference not to her aggressive volleying but to the fact that, like everyone else on the women's tennis tour, she plays in front of male spectators while wearing sleeveless tops and short skirts.

The clerics and their followers laid siege to the board's office in Raipur, the state capital, demanding the immediate withdrawal of the chapter.

"We cannot consider her a good Muslim because she exposes her body in front of male spectators," said Maolana Abu Bakkar Siddiqui, one of the clerics.

"Also, she went against the *sharia* [Islamic law], which forbids Muslim women being in games and sports. . . . No Muslim girl should be influenced by her non-Islamic way of life and no one should be encouraged to adopt her as a role model."

Mr. Khan later told police that he started to receive repeated telephone calls from people who refused to identify themselves but warned of "dire consequences" if the textbook went ahead as planned.

The strategy worked. "The pressure . . . was increasing every day. We had to decide to drop the chapter even after the proof was cleared for the press," he said. "We could not take any risk."

As soon as he backed down, the protests and threatening calls stopped, he added.

The episode is just the latest in a series involving Ms. Mirza, who started playing tennis when she was 6.

Famous, or Infamous?

When she returned home after participating in the U.S. Open [tennis tournament] last month [September 2005], she was swamped with accolades for being the first Indian woman to reach the fourth round in the prestigious competition (she lost to Russian sensation Maria Sharapova) as well as the first Indian woman to break into the top 50 of the world tennis rankings.

At the same time, clerics in her home city of Hyderabad issued a *fatwa* (religious decree) demanding that she cover up during matches. Her skirts and T-shirts, they said, are "un-Islamic" and "corrupting." (She had turned many heads at the tournament by appearing in a shirt that read: "I'm cute. No shit.")

Two weeks later, when she was getting ready for an international tournament in Calcutta, some Muslim leaders threatened to prevent her from playing if she showed up wearing a tight shirt and with her legs uncovered.

Authorities deployed hundreds of uniformed security agents and plainclothes officers around the Calcutta stadium where she played. Wherever she moved in the city, she was shadowed by commandos.

Ms. Mirza would rather avoid such controversy, saying the fact that everything she says or wears is now the subject of public discussion makes her uncomfortable.

"I follow all the tenets of Islam. I pray every day and read the Koran. I offer *zakat* [the 2.5 percent of their earnings that Muslims give to the poor] from my prize money. I fast during Ramzan [Ramadan] and will be going for *umrah* [a short pilgrimage to the holy city of Mecca] this month."

Her father, Imran Mirza, defends her: "I think what matters in Islam is whether one follows its five principles. The tennis uniform she wears should not be an issue at all."

Many moderate Muslim clerics and social leaders agree.

Muslim Women Are Held to Different Standards by Men

"Islam does not favour dressing up in a manner that draws attention," said Shaista Amber, president of All India Muslim Women's Personal Law Board. ". . . Sania, at least, has a reason. She dresses up in a particular manner so that she has better mobility on the court.

"But what about all those Bollywood males who unbutton their shirts at the drop of a hat or strut about in boxer shorts?

"Islam has always been generous to women. It is men who want to shackle women by making these unnecessary demands."

Even while she was the centre of so much controversy in Calcutta, senior Muslim leaders held a special meeting to discuss the *fatwa* against her and decided that she should not be put under any unwarranted pressure.

"It is impossible for a woman to play tennis at the international level dressed in long skirts and sleeves," said Hasan Imran, one of the leaders. "Those clerics did a mischief by issuing the *fatwa* against her."

And the Chhattisgarh *madrassa* board "made a blunder by withdrawing that chapter," he added.

Political commentator Rajdeep Sardesai said that, in Muslim society, all women can easily fall prey to religious prejudice, which only reinforces the persistent image of the Muslim as an evil, anti-woman obscurantist.

"Which is why being Sania Mirza in today's age is very important," he said. "She represents the empowered modern Indian woman's desire to be freed of the shackles of the past, expressing a joyous individuality that lies at the heart of the robust democratic society."

Or, as Mufti Shabbir Ahmed Siddiqui, a cleric in Ahmedabad, put it: "When this girl is making the country and the community proud with her performance, we should pardon her un-Islamic dress."

10

Homophobia in Male Professional Sports Is Encouraged by the Media

Joey Guerra

Joey Guerra is a columnist for the Houston Chronicle.

Although women's sports have begun to openly embrace their homosexual players and coaches, male athletics remains stubbornly resistant and reluctant to discuss the issue of sexuality—particularly that of its gay members. The media is partially responsible, but attitudes must also change from within the men's locker room before there can be any stronger level of acceptance and tolerance. Not only does the stereotypical negativity discourage players from coming out, it might also prevent some lucrative advertising in an increasingly open-minded business world.

The rough-and-tumble world of professional male sports, it seems, is the last bastion of homophobia in America. At least that's the overwhelming consensus of most U.S. media outlets.

Hardly a startling revelation, to be sure. But it's one that has been thrust into news reports and mainstream public consciousness in the wake of Houston Comets forward Sheryl Swoopes's decision to come out publicly. The three-time most valuable player for the Women's National Basketball Association [WNBA] has revealed that she has been in a romantic relationship with Alisa "Scotty" Scott, a former assistant coach for the Comets, for seven years.

The couple are raising Swoopes's 8-year-old son, Jordan. Swoopes was married to Jordan's father, football player Eric Jackson, until 1999.

Swoopes's decision to come out is commendable, but most sports websites, magazines and columnists agree that it's unlikely to make much difference for gay males in the professional sports world—an entirely different kind of beast.

"It's certainly admirable on (Swoopes's) part, but I don't think it's the sort of announcement that took anyone much by surprise. It was a pretty safe thing for her to say," says Ross von Metzke, entertainment editor for Hyperion Interactive Media, which runs the gaysports.com website.

Gay Male Athletes Face Ridicule

"Men in sports—it's still uncharted territory. Our stars are supposed to be masculine and heroic, or they are supposed to be almost asexual, where we know nothing about their sex lives. I'm not sure what will have to happen before that one becomes a safe announcement."

In a recent story on the subject, *Boston Herald* writer Mark Murphy illustrates a good example of the clear—and accepted—issue of homophobia in professional male sports.

"The culture of male athletics is built around the Jurassic notions of he-manhood, notions that don't jibe with the unfortunate stereotypes tethered to homosexuality."

He says, "The very mention of how Sheryl Swoopes and her groundbreaking announcement might apply to the NBA [National Basketball Association] jerked (Boston Celtics captain) Paul Pierce into abrupt laughter. What if . . . an NBA athlete—not necessarily a star—announced that he was gay? "I probably wouldn't want to guard him," Pierce is quoted as saying. Murphy adds that Pierce is "seemingly only half joking."

Unfortunately, that's the attitude most coaches and some players seem to be taking in response to the reality of gay men in professional sports. A public admission of homosexuality, the media says, just isn't something major-league sports is ready for, and they probably won't be ready for a very long time.

In his recent story in *The Journal News*, Ian O'Connor says, "the culture of male athletics is built around the Jurassic notions of he-manhood, notions that don't jibe with the unfortunate stereotypes tethered to homosexuality."

Homophobia Rules the Locker Room

By and large, the media seems to agree that professional male sports is a long way from acceptance of homosexuality—but many writers are also taking players and coaches to task for it.

Washington Post sports columnist Sally Jenkins, in her piece "Their Words of Discouragement," says, "Judging by some of the witless remarks in the sports world over the past few days, athletes and coaches are having a nationwide contest for Moron of the Week. The question becomes, should we ask these people about anything important, ever? Should we once and for all restrict the questions we put to sports figures to such matters as, what should the Red Sox do in the off-season, and, what are the merits of a [football defensive] 3–4 scheme versus the 4–3?"

In a recent article on Bloomberg.com, columnist Scott Soshnick says, "Athletes toss around slurs like rolled-up wads of discarded tape. Among jocks, it's the ultimate insult to insinuate that someone might be gay, which is probably why no male athlete has ever come out while still in uniform."

Ian O'Connor, a special contributor to FoxSports.com, also makes some powerful points in a recent column. "The more major sports leagues educate their players on this issue, the more likely it is that a gay athlete will emerge from the closet as eagerly as Jackie Robinson [the first African-American to play major-league baseball] pushed through the [Los Angeles] Dodgers clubhouse door," O'Connor says.

"Don't ask, don't tell is the prevailing law of the land."

But he is quick to add that, "Right now, no homosexual man currently playing in Major League Baseball, the NFL [National Football League], the NBA, or the NHL [National Hockey League] can take an honest survey of the landscape and know for sure that he'll be supported by his own team and league.

"Leagues and franchises are forever bringing in federal agents and counselors to warn players about the evils of gambling and drugs. They are forever preaching the need to practice responsible, safe sex. They are forever issuing alerts about the presence of the steroid police," O'Connor continues.

"But the subject of homosexuality in sports remains taboo, even though statistics and common sense suggest there are gay players in almost every locker room. Don't ask, don't tell is the prevailing law of the land."

Change Must Come From Within

Washington Post columnist Jenkins does, however, touch on an important aspect of the argument and blames more than just major-league players for the overwhelmingly negative stereotypes and myth[s] associated with gay men.

She says, "Athletes are increasingly separate from the rest of us—and we're all complicit in that fact. We identify them as stars as early as grade school, socialize them as privileged exceptions, pay them 25 times what the average person earns, and coach them to abdicate on social issues. So, it's no wonder that so many of them live in a bubble of self-absorption, and seem to think courage is demonstrated only on the field."

The media itself is largely to blame for the idolatry of sports figures, which in turn draws [a] deep line of separation between the "stars" and the "regular people" in the stands. But O'Connor's previously mentioned piece in *The Journal News* does include another interesting argument from Yvette Christofilis, executive director of a gay and lesbian community services center based in White Plains [New York]. "It's not the fans the gay player is probably worried about," Christofilis says, "I think it's the locker room, the organizations, the leaderships and the advertisers. I think most fans would applaud it."

It's about a football jock hanging with his friends at a swanky gay bar without being exposed by paparazzi.

The change, most media agrees, needs to first come from within the professional sports organizations, which stand steadfastly by the "Don't ask, don't tell" mantra. Fans will follow suit.

Male Athletics Stands to Gain by Acceptance

In the end, it's not only about making gay players feel comfortable enough to admit they are gay. It's about a male baseball player's partner or boyfriend cheering them on in the stands and a kiss after the big game. It's about a basketball player's serving as the grand marshall for a gay pride parade, with straight teammates in tow. It's about a football jock hanging with his friends at a swanky gay bar without being exposed by paparazzi.

And it's about all of these things happening while these players are still on major-league teams.

As for Swoopes, she says she does not expect to lose her lucrative endorsement deals with Nike and other companies. One of the reasons Swoopes says she has come out is an endorsement deal with Olivia Cruises and Resorts, the nation's most prominent lesbian-centered business.

Good for her. And maybe, just maybe, professional male athletes will get there someday.

11

Homosexuality Does Not Preclude Being an Athlete and Role Model

David Wharton

David Wharton has covered sports for the Los Angeles Times *for 25 years. His work has won a range of national honors, including the Associated Press Sports Editors award, and has been selected for* The Best American Sports Writing. *He is the author of two books on college football and has written for such magazines as* Surfer *and* Men's Fitness.

As a consequence of gradual social acceptance of homosexuality, more gay student-athletes are "coming out" and avowing their sexual preference. Although universal acceptance and/or tolerance is not guaranteed—and may never be—athletes who are honest about themselves are meeting far less resistance and hostility from their teammates than ever before. Encouraged by a mere handful of past players, most of whom did not dare come out until their professional days were over, today's openly gay athletes are paving the way toward greater understanding for themselves, their teammates, their opponents, and generations to follow.

The guys in his boat took to calling him "Badger" because of the grimace he wore during races. Part of a junior rowing club that ranked among the fastest in the nation, Lucas Goodman was relentless on the water.

It was a different story on land.

The teenager with the powerful build and close-set eyes had to be careful. He hung back ever so slightly when teammates shot the breeze, talking about girls.

"You get tired of constantly watching what you say, constantly watching how you act," he said. "You're almost paranoid."

Goodman felt so uneasy that he finally told the Green Lake Crew his secret: He is gay.

The 18-year-old belongs to an emerging generation of openly gay and lesbian athletes on high school and college campuses across the country. These young men and women are quietly venturing where no pro football or baseball star has gone, challenging the conformist, if not downright homophobic, tradition of the playing fields.

Their numbers are difficult to gauge because many confide only in peers. Experts chart the trend anecdotally through athletes who join gay rights clubs at school, e-mail gay rights advocates for advice or announce their sexual orientation on websites such as Facebook and MySpace.

"This is an issue that's in transition even as we speak," said Jay Coakley, a noted scholar and author on sports culture. "We're looking at how the world is changing."

Reactions Vary

Not all the stories have happy endings—a high school football player in northern California tells of being ostracized. But others, such as a Delaware runner and a Georgia hockey player, say they were welcomed by their teams.

Sociologists see the openness as a generational shift. Polls suggest a growing percentage of young people have more relaxed views about sexual orientation than their parents did.

In Seattle, Goodman began dropping hints around his eight-man boat more than a year ago. He talked with his best friend, and with another rower who seemed both understanding and physically large enough to make a good ally.

When word spread, no one teased or whispered about him. The crew saves money by sharing hotel beds on the road, and the teammate who bunks with Goodman didn't mind.

"So what if I sleep in the same bed with a straight guy or with Lucas?" Casey Ellis asked. "Either way, there's going to be another guy there with me."

Within a few weeks, Goodman figures, the surprise of his announcement wore off and "it ended up not being that big a deal."

Which is what makes his story, and others like it, a very big deal.

Openness Can Encourage Others

Allan Acevedo tends to speak hurriedly, words stacking up against each other. Finished with his morning run of three miles, sitting in a coffeehouse, the thin young man with dark sideburns rushes through a telling anecdote.

Two years ago, he and the rest of the track team from Bonita High School in La Verne [California] were talking idly before a meet.

"When I get married," he recalled saying, "the guy has to be—"

A teammate interrupted. "Did you say guy?"

"Oh," Acevedo replied. "You didn't know?"

Young athletes come out for various reasons. Goodman tired of pretending to like girls. Acevedo had something different in mind.

He volunteers for gay rights groups and said he once tried to enlist in the military to confront the "don't ask, don't tell" policy. When he insisted on telling, he said, the recruiter declined to complete his paperwork.

Acevedo joined the track team partly for love of the sport and partly to break stereotypes: "I wanted to say that I'm more than just gay."

Some teammates at Bonita High quietly switched aisles in the locker room, he said. Others seemed to run harder in practice, apparently determined not to lose to a gay guy.

Acevedo was undeterred and was open about his sexual orientation when he transferred to a Chula Vista school. At 18, he finds support in a development that encourages other young gay athletes: a shift in public opinion.

Attitudes Are Gradually Changing

A 2007 Gallup poll found that 57% of Americans viewed homosexuality as an "acceptable alternative lifestyle," an increase of 11 percentage points from four years ago. The percentage was higher among 18- to 29-year-olds.

Almost three-quarters of heterosexual adults said they would not change their feelings toward a favorite male athlete if he came out, according to a recent survey by Harris Interactive and Witeck-Combs Communications.

"It's not like the old days," said David Kopay, a former National Football League [NFL] player who stirred controversy by announcing he was homosexual in 1975.

Back then, gay athletes felt compelled to keep quiet, fearing hostile locker rooms and coaches who might cut them from the team.

Like Kopay, others waited until retirement to come out. In baseball, there were former Dodgers Glenn Burke and Billy Bean; in football, Roy Simmons of the Washington Redskins and, five years ago, Esera Tuaolo of the Green Bay Packers.

John Amaechi revealed his sexual orientation in a recent autobiography, *Man in the Middle*, published after he left the Utah Jazz of the National Basketball Assn. [NBA]. He sensed the change in attitude when he visited a Southern college campus during a promotional tour.

"A bunch of shirtless frat guys playing volleyball recognized me and started yelling," he said. "They were saying that they love what I'm doing."

Joey Fisher encountered a similar response at the University of Georgia, where his teammates recall thinking, *Wow, gay people play hockey?* when the goalie came out. No one mentioned anything to him at first.

But then, Fisher said, "about three days into training camp, one of my teammates tried to set me up with a friend of his. A guy."

Heterosexuals aren't the only ones acclimating to the idea of homosexuals in sports, Acevedo said. His gay friends were initially shocked when he ventured into the world of jocks.

"They said, 'You should wear a pink shirt,'" he recalled. "But then a lot of my friends went to my races."

"If they weren't going to accept me on the team . . . I wasn't going to stay."

Acevedo possesses a resilience common to athletes interviewed for this article. A fight with his parents—mainly over his sexual orientation—prompted him to move in with an older sister. He worked two jobs to support himself, which meant skipping track his senior year.

After graduating in the spring, he took a summer internship with a gay rights group in Washington, D.C., where he continues running on his own, staying in shape to try out for the team at San Diego State this fall.

"When I get there," he said, "I'll come out again."

Gay Female Athletes Face Different Challenges

There were no big announcements, no heartfelt talks in the locker room. As a freshman at Harvard, Sarah Vaillancourt simply decided to stop hiding her sexual orientation.

Whenever the subject of dating or relationships arose, she spoke frankly.

"If they weren't going to accept me on the team," she said, "I wasn't going to stay."

It helped that Vaillancourt quickly established herself among the top scorers on her college hockey squad and a rising star for Team Canada back home in Quebec. But she knew that as a lesbian, she would encounter challenges different from those facing gay male athletes.

On the plus side, she grew up with role models such as Billie Jean King and Martina Navratilova in tennis, Sheryl Swoopes in basketball and Rosie Jones in golf. Fans have come to expect a certain percentage of lesbians in women's sports.

This expectation also counts as a negative. In some circles, athletic women are automatically presumed to be lesbians, which can spark resentment among straight athletes.

Caitlin Cahow, a Harvard player and member of the U.S. women's hockey team, said: "Rumors get started and that makes everyone defensive about their sexuality, gay or straight. That's when it becomes a problem."

Vaillancourt, so candid at Harvard, acknowledges she is more cautious around the Canadian national team.

"They don't want me to talk about it so much, because if one person comes out, everyone's [going to be labeled] a lesbian," she said. "My whole team is not lesbian."

In college sports, negative recruiting is another concern. Some coaches try to scare high school prospects away from rival programs by suggesting those teams are predominantly lesbian. Kathy Olivier, the UCLA [University of California, Los Angeles] women's basketball coach, blames a hyper-competitiveness fueled by large coaching salaries.

"These are big-time positions," Olivier said. "I feel like some coaches would do anything."

At the University of Delaware, runner Lauren Stephenson said that coming out brought her closer to teammates.

Stephenson announced her sexual orientation as a junior, trying to soften the blow by saying she was bisexual. Soon, she found herself consoled in the locker room after a girlfriend cheated on her.

"All my teammates were telling me, 'You're so much hotter than she is, what is she thinking?'" Stephenson said. "It was just amazing."

Vaillancourt has had similar experiences in hockey, a sport she discovered as a toddler watching her brother play.

She has always been strong-willed, with a hint of defiance in her French Canadian accent and the arch of her eyebrows. Her parents worried when she came out in college.

"Being gay is only a small part of who I am."

"I know how people react sometimes," her mother, Monique, said. "People can be bad and mean."

Harvard players said they quickly warmed to Vaillancourt's wit and self-confidence and her straightforward manner in speaking about her sexual orientation. Off the team, some classmates did not react as kindly.

"I think it's because they don't have gay friends," said Laura Brady, a Harvard forward. "They just don't know."

Vaillancourt, now a 22-year-old junior, occasionally wonders about all the fuss. With so much of her time spent playing hockey and studying, "being gay is only a small part of who I am," she said.

In moments of impatience, she reminds herself that some people struggle to accept homosexuality for religious and other deep-seated reasons.

"You have to give people a chance to get used to all this," she said.

Gay High-school Athletes Face Resistance

The gym door was locked when Brian Schwind and his football teammates trudged off the practice field that day almost three years ago. As they waited for coaches with a key, Schwind realized he was surrounded.

The sophomore was new to Foothill High School near Redding [California]. By football standards he was smallish, a special teams player who stood only 5 feet 7. The larger players crowding around him demanded to know: Was he gay?

"Either I could tell the truth and have the crap beat out of me or I could lie and save myself," Schwind said. "My mom always told me to stand up for what I believe, so I told them."

A linebacker stepped in to prevent further trouble, but for the rest of the fall Schwind felt ostracized. After football, he went out for wrestling.

"Nobody wanted to wrestle with me," he recalled. "During weigh-ins, everybody was like, 'Get him out of the room.'"

His experience offers a reminder that poll numbers and television ratings for *Will & Grace* do not always translate to the schoolyard.

A 2005 survey by the Gay, Lesbian and Straight Education Network found that 64% of homosexual students had experienced some form of harassment in school. Gay rights groups cite higher suicide rates among homosexual teens, though the statistics are not universally accepted.

In sports, young gays face a paradox. The social status of playing athletics gives them a better chance of being accepted, but they must confront long-held biases.

The locker room can be especially tricky for boys. Corey Johnson, who in 1999 came out to his high school football team in Massachusetts, addressed the issue of shared showers and locker rooms head-on.

"I didn't touch you last year and I'm not going to do it this year," he told his teammates, adding: "And who says you guys are cute enough, anyway?"

The joke elicited a nervous ripple of laughter.

Adversity Affects Career Choices

At Washington University in St. Louis, Adam Goslin came out as a sophomore in 2004 and was welcomed by the football team. But the 6-foot-3, 220-pound defensive lineman often overheard teammates toss around homophobic slurs common to the locker room. Even players sensitive to his feelings could not always help themselves.

"I've had a couple of close friends tell me, 'I'm really trying not to, but I've been saying it for so many years and sometimes it slips out,'" he said.

The atmosphere confronting Schwind in Redding was more difficult.

Outed by the football team, he became more assertive, trying to form a club for gay students on the small-town campus. His efforts seemed to antagonize some athletes at a time when wrestling coach Jerry Vallotton was working hard to build Foothill High's program, with team unity a key element.

Schwind was new to the school, "and that in itself is difficult," Vallotton said in a recent interview. "Then if you carry a banner for another cause, whatever that cause may be, that's a double whammy."

"I want to be known as a rower . . . not as the gay kid."

The coach said he thought "all parties did the best they could."

By his junior year, Schwind gave up football and wrestling, sticking to swimming, where he felt more accepted. The experience has prompted him to consider a career in civil rights law.

"There can be a closed-minded shell around sports," he said. "Definitely, high school had a huge effect on my ideals about how things should be."

Acceptance Will Come About Gradually

When Lucas Goodman thought about coming out, he wasn't terribly concerned about acceptance—not as an accomplished rower and honors student headed to MIT [Massachusetts Institute of Technology] this fall. He knew that Seattle had a large gay population and that crew was "one of the most elitist liberal yuppie sports you could think of."

Goodman was more fearful that his sexual orientation might overshadow everything else.

"I want to be known as a rower," he said. "Not as the gay kid."

Gay rights advocates are just as eager for openly homosexual athletes to become so common that the issue fades away. That is why they place such hope in the new generation.

"A superstar coming out—I think it will happen, but I don't think that's how you create enormous change," said Johnson, the former high school football player, who now works as a media strategist for the Gay & Lesbian Alliance Against Defamation [GLAAD].

"You have enormous change with story after story about young people having positive experiences."

Goodman has already made a difference with the Green Lake Crew.

"Your impulse is not to talk about it because you don't know if that's private information or not," Coach Ed Maxwell said. "But the more you know and the more you understand about people who are different from you, the better off you are."

The experience has helped Goodman too.

He still rows fiercely, still bugs teammates about eating right and getting sleep before races. But now he is happier.

On a recent afternoon, the rowers shouldered their sleek boat to the edge of a small lake north of downtown. They were in a good mood after winning a silver medal at the U.S. Rowing Youth National Championship, joking and laughing, talking about parties.

It was the type of chatter that used to make Goodman nervous. Not anymore.

12

Athletes Need Training to Avoid Being the Targets of Troublemakers

Joseph Williams

Joseph Williams has been with the Boston Globe *for a total of ten years and has spent the last three of them in Washington, D.C. He left the* Globe *in 2003 to become an assistant managing editor with the* Star Tribune *in Minneapolis but returned to the* Globe *in 2005.*

In recent years, the number of gun-related incidents involving professional athletes has risen sharply. Wealth and fame cannot protect an athlete from potential harm—and in fact, can and do create a tempting target, especially when the athlete is socializing in popular nightclubs. When weapons enter the scene, albeit for purposes of self-protection, the danger worsens. Athletes, who are routinely offered education and training in other areas, need more guidance to address the issue.

Celtics star Paul Pierce is reluctant to discuss the night he nearly lost his life in a Boston nightclub eight years ago, but his skin tells part of the story: several small, nick-like scars on his cheek, a longer one under his right eye. The scars that mark his chest and back are hidden by his practice uniform.

At a morning practice here before a recent game against the Washington Wizards, Pierce was polite but terse when asked how he has changed since a group of men jumped him that night, beating him, stabbing him, and smashing a bottle over his head.

He would not say what he thought of Plaxico Burress, the New York Giants receiver who accidentally shot himself Nov. 28 with an unlicensed gun he brought into a Manhattan nightclub.

"I'm in a whole different situation [than Burress]," Pierce said. Though he said he's more careful "since I been through what I been through," he would not say how.

"That incident . . . I don't want to focus on that at all," Pierce said, abruptly waving his hand under his chin and cutting off the interview. "You want to talk about basketball, I'm good."

Yet Burress, who caught the winning touchdown in last season's Giants Super Bowl win over the Patriots, was in a similar situation as Pierce, the NBA's reigning Finals Most Valuable Player—both are young, highly paid star athletes whose night out with friends ended in a highly dangerous, potentially deadly situation.

By all accounts Pierce wasn't looking for trouble; Burress apparently armed himself in case anyone tried to attack him.

Experts in sports and society, however, say both cases point to a complex, stubborn problem in professional sports: athletes, particularly African-Americans, have become targets for criminals, leading some of them to arm themselves, increasing the possibility that something bad will happen to them or someone else.

An Alarming Trend

The arrest of Burress is the latest in a string of disturbing incidents involving pro athletes and violence.

On Jan. 1, 2007, drive-by gunmen shot and killed Broncos cornerback Darrent Williams after a confrontation in a downtown Denver nightclub on New Year's Eve; Williams was with NBA star Kenyon Martin and Oakland Raiders receiver Javon Walker at the time.

In October 2007, Adam "Pacman" Jones, an NFL star then with the Tennessee Titans, was allegedly involved in a fight and shooting at a Las Vegas strip club that wounded three people, leaving a club bouncer paralyzed.

In perhaps the highest-profile incident, Sean Taylor, a rising star with the NFL's Washington Redskins, was shot and killed in November 2007 in a home-invasion robbery in Miami.

And three months ago, Richard Collier, a lineman with the Jacksonville Jaguars, was paralyzed when assailants shot him 14 times as he headed home after a night out.

Both the NFL and the NBA have harshly punished players involved in off-field incidents; Jones, for example, was suspended for the entire 2007 season, forfeiting millions. Both leagues also feature mandatory player-education programs [to avoid bad situations by making better choices.

Some athletes steeped in urban or hip-hop culture can't or won't leave the expensive cars, jewelry, and oversized bankrolls behind.

"The real issue to me is when the players feel they're unsafe, they shouldn't be there," said NFL commissioner Roger Goodell days after Burress's arrest. "So, get out—don't be there. If you feel the need to have a firearm someplace, you're in the wrong place."

Learning Gap

But Dave Czesniuk, director of operations for Northeastern University's Center for the Study of Sport in Society, said

Goodell's comment misses the point. Most of the players in violent situations have been young African-Americans, something the league ignores in its player education.

"I think the huge gap lies in the makeup of players and makeup of management," said Czesniuk, who specializes in the relationship between race and sports. "There's a huge racial divide" between the NBA and the NFL leadership and the black athletes who dominate the leagues—and the culture some bring with them to the pros.

"A lot of times they aren't speaking the same language," he said.

While the majority of athletes in the NBA and the NFL avoid trouble, they do stand out by size alone, while their celebrity and high income make them appealing targets for troublemakers. The problem is compounded, Czesniuk said, when some athletes steeped in urban or hip-hop culture can't or won't leave the expensive cars, jewelry, and oversized bankrolls behind.

"That puts them in a position where they feel they need to defend themselves 'by any means necessary,'" including guns, Czesniuk said. "When they all come together you have the potential [for a dangerous situation]."

Former NFL star Jerome Bettis, who does commentary for NBC Sports, confirmed that viewpoint in a recent interview with the online website jocklife.com. "Some players like to splurge on very expensive items: rings, watches, bracelets, and chains," said Bettis, who played 13 seasons, mostly with the Pittsburgh Steelers. "So there have been a lot of instances where players have been robbed."

Christopher L. Henry, the NFL's director of player development, said the league is working to change those attitudes, particularly among new players who value a flashy lifestyle—and now have the money to get it.

"What we're looking at is young players coming into the league with practically 20 years of reinforced behavior," Henry said. "We're taking them out of their communities and giving them an opportunity that many of them have not seen before. With that comes a great responsibility."

Even if a player is trying to walk the straight and narrow, "People know everything about these guys—who they are, how much they make," Henry said. "It's a challenge, there's no question about that. Our job is to educate them about what they have to lose."

People, for better or worse, look up to athletes, so education is critical for everyone in our society.

Unfair Criticism

Richard Lapchick, an expert on sports culture, said he believes the NFL and NBA education programs are "absolutely imperative" to keep players out of trouble, but he said education should start even earlier, when a star player is in high school or college.

"The sooner you get to them the better off they'll be, either to stop themselves or intervene in a case where [violence] is happening," said Lapchick, director of the University of Central Florida's Sports Business Management program and a founder of Northeastern's Center for the Study of Sport in Society. "People, for better or worse, look up to athletes, so education is critical for everyone in our society."

Still, it's unfair to criticize athletes without examining American culture, which has become more violent in general, Lapchick said. Statistically, he said, a pro basketball or football player is no more likely to be involved in violent behavior, either as a perpetrator or a victim, than anyone else. "These individual athletes do have a problem, but it's a much bigger problem in America," he said.

Lapchick did agree that race plays a factor, but in perception of athletes as much as reality: critics are likely to tarnish black athletes in general if a pro football or basketball player is involved in an incident, but "when a hockey player or baseball player is arrested, I get calls about an individual athlete," Lapchick said.

Though the outpouring of support for Pierce as well as for the families of Williams and Taylor is touching, Lapchick said, scores more people die anonymously from violence nationwide on any given day.

Because they aren't athletes, he added, "We're never going to know their names. We're not going to support their families."

13

The Economic Downturn Will Return Sports to Its Former Purity

Simon Barnes

Simon Barnes is the longtime, award-winning chief sports columnist for the London Times. *His sports and nature columns are published in major newspapers throughout the United Kingdom.*

In recent times, sports and many of the athletes who perform or play them have been driven solely by monetary greed. Players' salaries are astronomical, and there has been virtually unlimited profitability through sponsorship in return for advertising and marketing rights. The glamour of rampant commercialism and consumerism has overtaken the most basic fundamentals of sport, which include playing for the sheer fun of competition and a desire to perform well in order to be victorious. As the economy falters, however, sport will survive—and will in fact be allowed to return to its former "purity" once the financial-gain factor is lessened or eliminated. The profiteers will abandon sport for other ventures, but true fans will remain and sport for its own sake will not only survive, but flourish.

I don't know if you've noticed, but something's gone a bit funny with money. One moment we were all doing very well: next minute we're all poor. It's as if a magic wand has been waved over the world, casting a great all-encompassing poor spell.

At once we must look for economies; well, best not cut down on bread and cheese and children's shoes. Better to economise on works of art, champagne, long-haul travel. Good things, favourite things, but life continues without them.

And sport. As people wonder about that season ticket, that pay-TV subscription, that trip to South Africa for 2010, so sport begins to panic. Sport is one of the things everyone can afford to do without. That's true for ordinary people, for billionaires, for local sponsors, for multinational companies.

So. All right then. Whither sport? There will certainly be changes—salary cuts, salary caps, closures, receivers, missing sponsors—but sport will also change from within. There is no avoiding this. Recession will force sport into some kind of moral alteration. Sport is in flux before our eyes: what form will it take as the financial changes become a fact rather than a threat?

Sports and Big Money

It seems a lifetime since [Texas billionaire] Allen Stanford was grinning his head off, pretending to be cricket's biggest-ever benefactor. Stanford is now talking about "reviewing" his commitment to cricket less than a year into a five-year deal. [Car manufacturer] Honda has pulled out of Formula One, Subaru from motor rallying. [Cellular service] Vodafone has left [British soccer team] Manchester United and is leaving the England cricket team. Liverpool is just one football club in a spin (what will happen if the Royal Bank of Scotland, now part government-owned, won't renegotiate its loan?). The British Government is cutting back on Olympic funding.

Suddenly, sport is no longer sexy. Suddenly, the gorgeous, pouting minx of sport has found that no one fancies her any more, or at least, they have stopped stuffing banknotes down her cleavage. What's a girl supposed to do in such circumstances?

Sport has for years been sashaying across the world, playing off one admirer against another, utterly confident that there was always plenty more where that came from. Now, with shocking suddenness, everything has changed. Sport's priorities cannot help but change with everything else. Sport sucked in thousands of people who love money (and such related items as prestige and power and glamour) far more than they ever loved sport. For such people, sport is now infinitely less interesting.

Sport doesn't need billions to survive.

Too Much Emphasis on Money

Those who cosied up to soccer because it is full of consumer-cool, to rugby because it speaks to young middle-class blokes with disposable income, to cricket because of the Asian markets, are finding sport substantially less thrilling than it was a few weeks ago.

There has been a dramatic change in the relationship between sport and money. But if sport is a lot less attractive to people fascinated by money, it is as attractive as ever to people fascinated by sport. Sport doesn't need billions to survive. All it needs is us: people who are stupid enough to care about it.

How will sport cope with this changed landscape, one without the lofty mountains of prestige and the deep valleys flowing with milk and money? Will recession create a new amateurism? Will the outmoded virtues of more austere times come surging back? Will sport create a 21st century *Chariots of Fire* [a film based on British athletes in the 1924 Summer Olympics]?

Er, no. History doesn't have a reverse gear. The society that produces sport today is radically different from the society that produced [British track stars] Harold Abrahams, Eric Liddell and Lord Lindsay. If sport returns to comparative poverty, it will do so in a 21st century way. And while for some, the quest for money gets even more desperate, for others, not necessarily the rich, there is a highly significant opportunity to relegate money down the hierarchy of priorities.

Inevitably, there will be less emphasis on marketing. Perhaps a miracle will take place and people who run, say, the England cricket team will stop referring to it as "the product."

Sport Will Return to Basics

Perhaps, in these straitened times, those who run sport will be forced to consider the possibility that the value of sport is rather different from the price. In its recent years of head-spinning prosperity, sport has not played hard to get. In fact, it has flung itself on every kerb-crawler [a person who solicits business from prostitutes] like Julia Roberts at the start of *Pretty Woman*. Every sport in the calendar has done everything it can to sell itself to the moneymen. The penalty shoot-out turns soccer into a TV game show and cricket is selling the most beguilingly complex sporting form in the world down the river.

But when sport gets its hands on money, it all goes on fripperies and vanities and one-upmanship: unheard-of salaries, dizzying transfers, fleets of experts with no comprehensible form of expertise.

If people are no longer in sport for the money, then they must be in it for something else.

All that money that has been so briefly a part of sport, and all gone on [British soccer star] Cristiano Ronaldo's hair gel. Sport has rarely spent its own money, preferring to squander it. The money's come, the money's going fast, yet sport remains. That's the point to hold on to. There is [traditional]

Test cricket to watch, a meaty Christmas program of soccer, a new year with the [cricket team] Ashes and [Jamaican runner] Usain Bolt.

Sport will survive, not because it will find more money, but because it can rely on the will of sporting kind. It may even become a more satisfying thing as a result. We won't see a return to a Golden Age of Corinthianism [an era of celebration and plenty], but there is an opportunity to see things that have for years been hidden by chequebooks and piles of cash and IOUs and goodie bags and freebies.

Sport Will Be Revitalized

Some kind of new start is possible. We can stop prizing sport because of the amount of money if makes and start prizing it because of other less readily computable things. If people are no longer in sport for the money, then they must be in it for something else. It would not be a bad idea for everyone in sport to realise this.

If so, we might be spared such things as sports agents, the notion that salary is an exact measure of personal worth, Stanford and his box of billions, Formula One's oil-drunk arrogance, [pro golfer] Tiger Woods' endorsements, the prostration before the gods of television, at least some of the temptation to take drugs. There are things that sport can afford to lose.

And the more we lose, the more we realise that what remains is what matters, and what matters is the action, and with it the narrative. What remains, when the accountant has finished his work on the past year in sport, is not the millions gained and lost and the buying and the selling and the earning and the sacking. What remains is Usain Bolt's run, [race driver] Lewis Hamilton's last corner, [Spanish tennis star] Rafael Nadal's forehand and [American swimmer] Michael Phelps' stroke. Is this altogether the disaster the moneymen think it is?

Organizations to Contact

The editors have compiled the following list of organizations concerned with the issues debated in this book. The descriptions are derived from materials provided by the organizations. All have publications or information available for interested readers. The list was compiled on the date of publication of the present volume; the information provided here may change. Be aware that many organizations take several weeks or longer to respond to inquiries, so allow as much time as possible.

Cal Ripken, Sr. Foundation
1427 Clarkview Road, Suite 100, Baltimore, MD   21209
(410) 823-0808 • fax: (443) 841-7033
Web site: www.ripkenfoundation.org

A nonprofit organization, the Cal Ripken, Sr. Foundation helps to build character and teach critical life lessons to disadvantaged young people residing in America's most distressed communities through baseball- and softball-themed programs.

Center for the Study of Sport in Society
Northeastern University, Boston, MA   02115
(617) 373-4025 • fax: (617) 373-4566
Web site: www.sportinsociety.org

The center is a social justice organization that uses sport to create social change by working locally, nationally, and internationally to promote physical activity, health, violence prevention, and diversity among young people, adults, and college and professional athletes.

Coalition of Intercollegiate Athletics (COIA)
2009 Co-Chair Professor Nathan Tublitz, Eugene, OR   97403
(541) 346-4510
Web site: www.neuro.uoregon.edu/~tublitz/COIA/index.html

COIA was formed in 2002 and is an alliance of faculty senates from 55 Division 1-A universities. The independent organization promotes comprehensive reform of intercollegiate athletics.

The Drake Group
Contact can be made via e-mail: info@thedrakegroup.org
Web site: www.thedrakegroup.org

The mission of the Drake Group is to help college faculty and staff to defend academic integrity in the face of the burgeoning college sport industry. The group lobbies for proposals that ensure quality education for college athletes, supports faculty whose job security is threatened for defending academic standards, and provides information on current issues involving sports and higher education.

Gay & Lesbian Athletics Foundation (GLAF)
PO Box 425034, Cambridge, MA   02142
(617) 588-0600 • fax: (617) 588-0600
Web site: www.glaf.org

GLAF promotes acceptance and visibility of the gay, lesbian, bisexual, and transgendered athletics community through education; mentoring; training; support networks; promotion of positive role models and healthy lifestyles; and advocating for inclusion, recognition, understanding, and respect among all age levels in competitive sports.

Knight Commission on Intercollegiate Athletics
Executive Director, Amy Perko
(910) 864-5782
Contact can be made with the commission through its Web site: www.knightcommission.org

Formed in 1989, the Knight Commission has sought to be an agent of change in trying to reconnect college sports with the educational mission of America's colleges and universities. The commission also encourages faculty members at colleges to become involved in issues involving athletics.

The Miami Project to Cure Paralysis
P.O. Box 016960 (R-48), Miami, FL   33101-6960
(305) 243-6001 • fax: (305) 243-6017
Web site: www.miamiproject.miami.edu

In 1985, Barth A. Green, M.D., and NFL Hall of Fame line-backer Nick Buoniconti helped found The Miami Project to Cure Paralysis after Nick's son, Marc, sustained a spinal cord injury during a college football game. Today, The Miami Project is the world's largest, most comprehensive spinal cord injury research center, boasting an international team of more than 200 scientists, researchers, and clinicians.

National Collegiate Athletic Association (NCAA)
National Office, Indianapolis, Indiana   46206-6222
(317) 917-6222 • fax: (317) 917-6888
Web site: www.ncaa.org

The NCAA is a voluntary organization through which the nation's colleges and universities govern their athletic programs. More than 1,000 academic institutions are members of the NCAA. The NCAA's stated core purpose is to, among other things, "integrate intercollegiate athletics into higher education so that the educational experience of the student-athlete is paramount."

Special Olympics
1133 19th Street NW, Washington, DC   20036-3604
(202) 628-3630 • fax: (202) 824-0200
Web site: www.specialolympics.org

Since 1968, the Special Olympics and its competitive athletes have been bringing one message to the world: people with intellectual disabilities can and will succeed if given the opportunity. Special Olympics understands the value of involving young people in its movement. By educating youth that intellectual disabilities cross all boundaries of age, gender, religion, and culture, and showing them that all people have something to contribute, Special Olympics is building communities of acceptance for the next generation. Special Olympics provides opportunities to get involved with Unified Sports, through Special Olympics Get Into It® curriculum and Youth Summits for communal conversations about acceptance and change.

Women's Sports Foundation
Eisenhower Park, 1899 Hempstead Turnpike, Suite 400
East Meadow, NY   11554
(800) 227-3988 • fax: (516) 542-4716
Web site: www.womenssportsfoundation.org

Founded by Billie Jean King in 1974, the mission of the Women's Sports Foundation is to advance the lives of girls and women through sport and physical activity.

Bibliography

Books

Jerome Bettis
The Bus: My Life in and out of a Helmet. NY: Doubleday, 2007.

Oscar
De La Hoya
American Son: My Story. NY: HarperCollins, 2008.

Bonnie Hinman
Xtreme Athletes: Danica Patrick. Greensboro, NC: Morgan Reynolds Publishing, 2009.

Greg Hoard
Joe: Rounding Third and Heading for Home. Wilmington, OH: Orange Frazer Press, 2004.

Billie Jean King
Pressure is a Privilege: Lessons I've Learned from Life and the Battle of the Sexes. NY: LifeTime Media, 2008.

Vince Papale
Invincible: My Journey from Fan to NFL Team Captain. NY: Hyperion, 2006.

Danica Patrick
Crossing the Line. NY: Simon and Schuster, 2006.

Pete Sampras
A Champion's Mind: Lessons from a Life in Tennis. NY: Crown Publishers, 2008.

Mary Tillman
Boots on the Ground By Dusk: My Tribute to Pat Tillman. NY: Rodale, Inc., 2008.

| John Edgar Wideman | *Fatheralong: A Meditation on Fathers and Sons, Race and Society.* NY: Pantheon Books, 1994. |

Periodicals

Arizona Republic staff	"What Does Marion Jones' Fall from Grace Say About Our Win-at-All-Cost Ethic?" *Arizona Republic*, October 8, 2007.
Mark Bradley	"A Reason for Hope Still There for Vick," *Atlanta Journal-Constitution*, May 21, 2009.
Eileen Brennan	"Ask Tim Tebow: Religion and Football Can Co-exist," *USA Today*, January 14, 2009.
Tom Chiarella	"Just Throw the Damn Ball, Tom Brady," *Esquire*, August 6, 2008.
Paul Daugherty	"Rose-Colored Glasses Cloud Truth for Roger Clemens," *The Cincinnati Enquirer*, May 12, 2009.
Amy Donaldson	"Do Men Really Take Danica Patrick Seriously?" *Deseret News*, October 25, 2006.
Mike Fish	"Donaghy's Father Says NBA Must Share the Blame," *ESPN the Magazine*, July 29, 2008.
Sean Gregory	"Feeling Betrayed by Marion Jones," *Time*, October 5, 2007.

Laura Kaminker	"2007 Person of the Year: Chantal Peticlerc," *New Mobility Magazine*, January 2008.
Gwen Knapp	"It's a Good Time for McGwire to Come Clean," *San Francisco Chronicle*, January 15, 2009.
Mike Lopresti	"A-Rod Fairy Tale Career Takes Disturbing Turn," *USA Today*, February 8, 2009.
Peter Schmuck	"With Ripken, Gwynn, Town Has True Legends," *Baltimore Sun*, July 28, 2007.
Gary Smith	"Pat Tillman: Remember His Name," *Sports Illustrated*, September 5, 2006.
Mark Starr	"To An Athlete Dying Young," *Newsweek*, November 27, 2007.
George Vecsey	"Phelps Needs Less Idle Time, Not More," *New York Times*, February 6, 2009.

Index